Getting Things Done
Through Project Management

Deji Badiru

ABICS Publications
A Division of
AB International Consulting Services

iUniverse, Inc.
New York   Bloomington

Getting Things Done Throught Project Management

iUniverse books may be ordered through booksellers or by contacting:

iUniverse
1663 Liberty Drive
Bloomington, IN 47403
www.iuniverse.com
1-800-Authors (1-800-288-4677)

ISBN: 978-1-4401-3822-5 (sc)
ISBN: 978-1-4401-3823-2 (ebook)

Printed in the United States of America

iUniverse rev. date: 4/30/2009

Dedication and Celebration

This book is dedicated to all the bubbly beings who espouse the spirit of positive thinking; for they shall succeed with their projects. They feel no evil, think no evil, see no evil, hear no evil, and speak no evil. They perceive silver lining and positives in everything. They always celebrate the success of a project with smiles and festivity.

Preface

In this book, the author brings the proven tools and techniques of project management from the corporate world to the pedestrian and common-user level for practical street-wise application to both personal and professional pursuits. The book is designed as a self-help resource and self-paced guide. It provides step-by-step guide for getting things done.

Project management has several underlying philosophies, principles, and epithets as motivation for executing a project. Following a project plan creates an atmosphere of progress toward an eventual goal in terms of incremental steps, recognized as tasks and activities. Taken together, the set of activities constitutes an identifiable project that can be managed with corporate-oriented techniques of project management. Any of the standard self-help guides and self-development pieces of advice can fit into the overall repertoire of project management methodologies.

Reflecting the author's artistic interests, the book has generous embedding of figures and diagrams to illustrate applications of project management concepts. Topics covered include project planning, project organizing, scheduling, project monitoring, progress tracking, control, and close-out. Guiding and motivational philosophies also abound throughout the book.

Deji Badiru
March 2009

Chapter One

Introduction to Getting Things Done

"I like work. It fascinates me. I can sit and look at it for hours."
                                                    - Jerome Klapka Jerome

===

Does it not sound ironic that nowadays, we plan more, but we always seem to accomplish less? That is often because we plan more than what we can deliver. Well, project management can help rectify this dilemma.

No matter your gender, age, creed, religion, or profession, you need project management to get things done. The faster and more effectively you carry out your tasks, the more time you'll have for all the other important activities in your life – love, family, friends, Church, school, travel, fun, and so on.

If practiced "religiously," as this author has done for years, project management allows you to do more in a shorter period of time.

Unless you are like Jerome K. Jerome, who expatiates his famous quote by saying "I love to keep it (work) by me. The idea of getting rid of it (getting it done) nearly breaks my heart."

The basic advice of this book is to:

Just Git'r Done!

No excuses. Just get done what needs done. This book is about "getting things done" through the techniques of project management. It is about making a difference in accomplishing goals; whether it is at home or at work. Whatever it is, just get it done or "Git'r Done" like they say in one familiar neighborhood. Procrastination is not in the vocabulary of project management. The techniques presented in this book can help readers to manage deadlines and track projects successfully. The techniques and suggestions can be put to use immediately to generate results.

It is a fact that managing projects effectively at home or at work can lead to a more balanced, happy, and healthy life; devoid of stress. If you are sick and tired of not getting enough done, you need project management.

A journal subscription renewal notice from *The Chronicle of Higher Education* says, "Life is full of deadlines. You meet them, beat them, perhaps even miss them, but you know better than to ignore them." This is a terse and pungent statement that is, indeed, very true. Deadlines that are missed simply come back to haunt us later on; causing more time and often leading to a higher cost; not to talk of the stress of embarrassment.

It is general knowledge that those who can get things done will always succeed with their goals and aspirations. "Things" that must be done are the building blocks of goals and objectives. Thus, accomplishing those building blocks moves us closer to our goals and objectives.

Someone once said,

"Projects would run well if people did not get in the way."

So, get out of the way of your project and get it done. In other words, don't encumber your projects with your own personal operational incompetence.

Exercise Self-Commitment

The single most important requirement for getting things done is self-commitment. It is through the discipline of self-commitment that projects, both large and small, can be executed successfully.

Without self-commitment to do what needs to be done when it needs to be done, nothing can be accomplished satisfactorily. As a case in point, the number of those getting project management training and certification is increasing rapidly. Yet, the number of project failures, with significant cost, schedule, and performance implications, is also increasing. This is a fact that is inconsistent with theory and conventional expectation. If there is no self-commitment to execute a project according to plan, no amount of education, training, credentialing, tools, and techniques can rescue the project. Those who are most eloquent about what needs to be done, and how, are often the ones who falter when it comes to actually doing it. Each person must self-dedicate and self-actuate to make commitment to get things done the way they ought to be done. The author's equation of success shown below is applicable in this regard.

Use Badiru's Equation of Success

Success is a function of three variables with the mathematical relationship below:

$$S = f(x, y, z)$$

where:

x = Intelligence: Intelligence is an innate attribute, which every one of us is endowed with.

y = Common Sense: Common sense is an acquired trait, which we learn from our everyday social interactions.

z = Self-Discipline: Self-discipline is an inner drive (personal control), which helps an individual to combine common sense with intelligence so as to achieve success.

With this equation, project success is within reach. Projects cannot succeed on intelligence alone. We must use common sense and self-commitment and discipline to facilitate success in getting things done.

One instance of lack of self-control often leads to recurring regrets and distraction from real project goals. One minute of indiscretion, under the guise of "enjoyment," can lead to everlasting sorrow and project failure.

Initiate Success

Achieving success with getting things done is actually simple, if one initiates success right from the beginning. All it takes are a few key ground rules and perseverance, such as those listed below:

- Exercising commitment
- Exhibiting fortitude
- Extending compromise
- Demonstrating selectivity in what is persued
- Embracing delegation when appropriate
- Displaying diligence
- Showing perseverance
- Teaming and partnering through:
  - Communication
  - Cooperation
  - Coordination
- Using the right tools
- Timing of what is done
- Outsourcing what is better done elsewhere

Maximize the utilization of each available hour of each day. Do, during the day, what you need daylight or working hours to do. Conversely, do not do, during the day, what you don't need daylight or working hours to do. In other words, use daylight hours appropriately to perform tasks that truly need daylight hours and put off until after-hours, those things that can be done at off hours.

Outsource tasks for which you have no skills, tools, or time; or from which you do not derive enjoyment or gratification. But you must retain control of accountability for the tasks.

Get the Right Help

In order to do certain types of projects right, you must get the right person to do it. Don't over-indulge in DIY (Do-It-Yourself) mentality on all things. Some things are better done by those who know what they are doing; and those who have the right tools. The comic in Figure 1.1 emphasizes the need for assigning tasks to qualified people.

Even good projects can go bad for several reasons including the following:

- Ineffective management of requirements
- Inadequate risk appreciation and management
- Improper scope management
- Lack of full commitment
- Lack of streamlining
- Unrealistic expectations
- Action bluffing with no real action (see explanation below)

Figure 1.1: Get the Right Person to the Job
(Reprinted with Permissions: LOCKHORNS © WM Hoest
Enterprises, Inc. King Features Syndicate)

Use Personal Care for Project Care

Many little choices that we make about what we do or don't do ultimately affect execution of projects. Make healthy personal choices; and you remain healthy to execute your projects successfully. Make personal bad choices, and they will come back to haunt you. Poor health and sour outlook impede the ability to execute projects efficiently.

Take Care of yourself so that you can take of your projects.

Likewise, take care of your means of transportation. Take care of your car so that you can get to where you need to be promptly to do what you need to do in a timely manner. Many of our projects these days depend on accessible modes of transportation. Thus, project implementation can be very car-dependent. Getting to work on time, arriving on time for appointments, reaching a destination safe all can be impacted by the operational condition of our vehicles. For example, if we get our vehicles ready for harsh winter conditions, we will experience fewer car-related project delays. Winter transportation problems can be preempted by getting our cars ready for winter by doing the following:

- Service and maintain radiator system
- Replace windshield-wiper fluid with appropriate winter mixture
- Check tire pressure regularly
- Invest in replacing worn tires
- Maintain full tank of fuel during winter months to keep ice from forming in the tank and fuel lines
- Have ice scrapers accessible in the within passenger space in the vehicle; not stored in the trunk

Practice Self Regulation

Have you ever considered yourself as a resource for your projects? That is, a resource that should be managed and regulated? Taking care of oneself is a direct example of human resource management, which is crucial for project success. Proper diet, exercise, and sleep are essential for mental alertness and positively impact the ability to get things done. Sleep, for example, affects many aspects of mental and physical activities. Sleep more and you will be amazed that you can get more done. This is because being well rested translates to fewer errors and preempts the need for rejects and rework. The notion that you have to stay up to get more done is not necessarily always true. Likewise, keep fit and get more done. Studies have confirmed that fit kids get better grades in school. Similarly, fit adults have been found to advance more professionally.

Avoid Action Bluffing

It is imperative to avoid "management by bluffing." It is not always easy to accomplish what you "bluff" to do. Thus, cutting down on "action bluffing" and being selective with pledges will help streamline the list of things to do. Like one IBM T.V. commercial says, "Stop talking. Start doing." This statement suggests the need to move on to the implementation stage of what needs to be done. Plans formulated so beautifully on paper or articulated in words mean nothing if they cannot be implemented.

In addition to overall strategies for getting to where we want to be, there must be tactical actions for getting there. This, essentially, is the purpose of project management. Project management is about creating the building blocks, called Work Breakdown Structure (WBS), that serve as steps toward the eventual project goal. Each element of the WBS represents something that must be done. Project management helps in getting those things done. That means we get things done through project management. WBS facilitates breaking a project up into manageable chunks. Project partition or segmentation improves overall project control at the operational level.

It is a fact that success can only be assured through dealing with manageable sets of tasks and activities. Whenever possible, consolidate activities. If we attempt to tackle multi-dimensional solutions that will require many players and participants, it would be more difficult to get everything to come together.

Develop a Strategy

Strategy is the vehicle for closing the gap between the current state and a desired future state. In order to build an effective strategy, we must have a honest assessment of the current state and a realistic evaluation of what can be achieved from that current state. For example, if current annual income is $75,000.00 and it is desirable to move up to $85,000.00, a strategy must be developed to close that gap. It is obvious that the strategy to be developed will be a function of the two end-points. If the disjoint between the two end points cannot be resolved, no amount of strategizing can close the inherent gap. Once a strategy has been formulated, the techniques of project management will be needed to actually implement the strategy. Thus, Strategy Building and Project Management are intimately tied together. They jointly produce desired results as shown in the linkage below:

Strategy Building ⬅==➔ Project Management ➔➔ Results

Project management is the vehicle of strategy. You cannot have a strategy without project management. Likewise, you cannot have project management without it being tied to a strategy. In the corporate world, much is made of the process of business strategy development; without a concerted effort toward project management. No wonder many corporate strategies fail.

In between strategy and project management lie risks. Every endeavor is subject to risks. If there were no risks, there would be no actions. Risks create opportunities. We must appreciate the risks that our projects portend and develop appropriate strategies to mitigate the risks. We must learn to strategize, streamline, and integrate project activities as shown in Figure 1.2.

Figure 1.2: Strategize, streamline, and integrate activities

Consider Time-Cost-Quality Tradeoffs

Always weigh cost versus time, cost versus quality, and time versus quality. Preempt problems by using multi-dimensional decision analysis. A simple example is a trade-off decision analysis of traveling by air or by road. The objective here is to get the travel done subject to the nuances of cost, time, and quality; which form the so-called Iron Triangle. The concept of Iron Triangle, also known as Triple Constraints, examines the trade-offs between cost, time, and quality or budget, schedule, and performance. The cliché in this respect is "cost, time, quality; which two do you want?" This implies that all three cannot be satisfied at equal levels. So, a trade-off or compromise must be exercised. This is shown graphically in Figure 1.3.

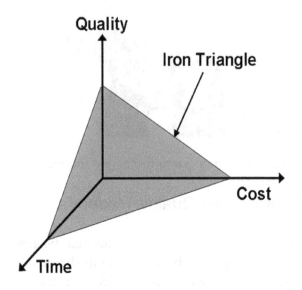

Figure 1.3: Iron Triangle Trade-Off within the Triple Constraints

As factors of importance in iron triangle decision analysis, the pros and cons of air travel and road travel are summarized below. Of course, each traveler will have to consider his or her own value streams, risk tolerance level, risk aversion, and goals in the process of making the best decision within the prevailing scenario.

Advantages of Air Travel over Road Travel

- Faster
- Statistically safer
- Less tiring

Advantages of Road Travel over Air Travel

- Flexible (depart at your leisure)
- Less travel hassles
- Often cheaper than air fare
- No airport parking worries
- No airport security lines to worry about
- No incidental expenses, car rental, or taxi

- Reduced weather sensitivity
- Ability to pack and take more
- Better meal planning at preferred stopping points
- Ability to take rest stops when needed
- Comfort of the vehicle compared to restricted airplane sitting options
- Pet-friendly
- Protection from unknown seat mates
- No cancellation penalty
- Safety is more within the control of the driver. While flying is said to be statistically safer than driving, there are several things that the road driver can do to increase road safety dramatically.

Case Example of Problem Avoidance

In over 30 years of driving on local, rural, back-road, and interstate roadways all over the USA, this author has never been involved in any type of accident (knock on wood); not even fender-benders. He has defensive and avoidance driving habits to avert being involved in accidents. Simple practices such as not following too close, not over-speeding, and being courteous to other drivers can significantly increase the chances of not being involved in an accident. It "takes two to tangle," and if one partner is unwilling and uncooperative in the tangling act, road collisions can be minimized. The last time this author was pulled over for traffic offense was in 1982 on Interstate 75 somewhere in Georgia, doing 71 where 55 was the limit. He still believes the stoppage was unjustified and was instigated by the fact that he was driving his beloved "hot rod" aka 1976 Chevy Camaro Rally Sport (shown in Figure 1.4). He vowed since then never to allow himself to be subject to any other unjustified traffic pull-over. He has respected and honored that vow ever since. He refers to his conservative driving habits as simply "respecting yourself" so that others can respect your space and time.

Figure 1.4: 1976 Camaro Rally Sport (Time and Functionality)

A couple of hours spent attending to being stopped by a state trooper or sorting out accidents details are hours taken away from some other projects. Over the years, this author has been asked how he manages to get so many things done so effortlessly. His usual response is "project management." This simply means using problem preemption techniques to avoid distractions that impede desired projects. Problem avoidance makes it possible to devote time to and focus on activities that really matter for project execution purposes.

Play by the Rule

Haste makes waste and rush makes crash. Playing by the rule up front saves time later on to get things done. Circumventing rules to cut corners can only lead to distractions and the need for time-consuming amendment later on. Time and effort invested in complying with rules and conforming to order pays off in the long run. The author describes himself as being a "self-imposed compliant conformist." This is a strategy that works by preempting trouble spots that would otherwise require resolution time. There will sometimes be a need for more time-consuming prudence in dotting all i's and crossing all t's before concluding a deal, whatever the "deal" might be. If the prudence is not exercised upfront, it may come back to cause project distractions and delays later on.

Get on with It

In the final analysis of getting things done, the basic approach is to get on with it. There is never a perfect time to get something done. Each opportunity comes with its own constraints. Each constraint may entail its own certain level of necessity. This may be necessity that must be attended to; such that avoiding the constraints is not possible. If one waits for the perfect time, most things will never get done. We must be willing to compromise, accept trade-offs, and move on.

Chapter Two

Project Management Fundamentals

"Give me six hours to chop down a tree and I will spend the first four sharpening the axe."

- Abraham Lincoln

With the quote above, Abraham Lincoln pointed out the utmost importance of doing the first thing first, in order to accomplish the overall goal more expediently. Project management is a structured approach to getting things done while using tools and resources effectively. The world has become very inter-connected and project management represents a common language of operation for creating products, providing services, and achieving results. "Sharpening your axe" means sharpening your mind and getting your resources aligned with your goals. In technical terms, this author defines project management as follows:

> "Project management is the process of managing, allocating, and timing resources to accomplish objectives in an efficient and expeditious manner."

Managing projects is not about working harder; it is about working smarter, securing the right tools, and making sure that the tools are in peak working condition. Even quite ubiquitous tools such as faulty writing pens or dull kitchen knives pose obstacles to smooth and expeditious actions.

Foundation for Project Success

In this book, we will focus on applying the above definition to personal projects. The same operational strategies that corporations employ are the same that individuals can employ to realize the benefits of project management in their personal pursuits. In fact, as it is often said that "charity begins at home," personal application of project management techniques are essential for corporate leaders in making disciplined decisions about business operations. Practicing project management for personal activities prepares an individual for corporate application and vice versa. The gear of project success requires integrating functions and objectives such that endeavors are complementary of one another.

In order to build a foundation for project success, we must determine where each item fits and integrate it into the overall requirements of a project.

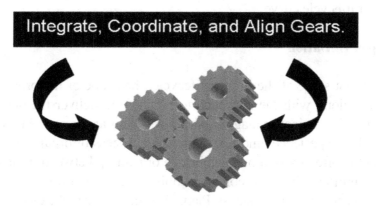

Integrate, Coordinate, and Align Gears.

Steps of Project Management

The objectives of a project may be stated in terms of time (schedule), performance (quality), or cost (budget). Time is often the most critical aspect of managing any project. Time must be managed concurrently with all other important aspects of any project, particularly in an academic setting. Project management covers the basic stages listed below:

1. Initiation
2. Planning
3. Execution

4. Tracking and Control
5. Closure

The stages are often contracted or expanded based on the needs of the specific project. They can also overlap based on prevailing project scenarios. For example, tracking and control often occur concurrently with project execution. Embedded within execution is the function of activity scheduling. If contracted, the list of stages may include only Planning, Organizing, Scheduling, and Control. In this case, closure is seen as a control action. If expanded, the list may include additional explicit stages such as Conceptualization, Scoping, Resource Allocation, and Reporting. Figure 2.1 shows the typical steps of project management while Figure 2.2 illustrates a plot of the project lifecycle curve.

Project Initiation

In the first stage of the project lifecycle, the scope of the project is defined along with the approach to be taken to deliver the desired results. The project manager and project team are appointed based on skills, experience, and relevance. The process of organizing the project is often carried out as a bridge or overlap between initiation and planning. The most common tools used in the initiation stage are Project Charter, Business Plan, Project Framework, Overview, Process Mapping, Business Case Justification, and Milestone Reviews. Project initiation normally takes place after problem identification and project definition.

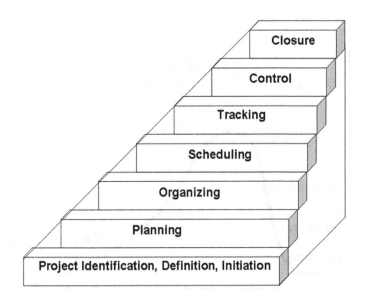

Figure 2.1: Steps of Project Management

Project Planning

The second stage of the project lifecycle includes a detailed identification and assignment of tasks making up the project. It should also include a risk analysis and a definition of criteria for the successful completion of each deliverable. During planning, the management process is defined, stakeholders are identified, reporting frequency is established, and communication channels are agreed upon. The most common tools used in the planning stage are Brainstorming, Business Plan, Process Mapping, and Milestones Reviews.

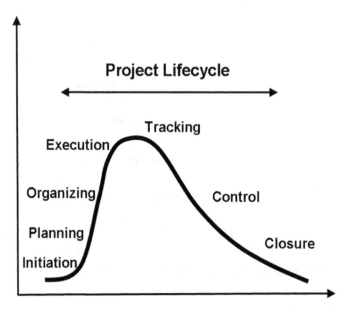

Figure 2.2: Stages within Project Lifecycle Curve

Execution and Control

The most important issue in the execution and control stages of the project lifecycle involves ensuring that tasks are executed expeditiously in accordance with the project plan, which is always subject to re-planning. Tracking is an implicit component and prerequisite for project control. For projects that are organized for producing physical products, a design resulting in a specific set of product requirements is created. The integrity of the product is assured through prototypes, validation, verification, and testing. As the execution phase progresses, groups across the organization become progressively involved in the realization of the project objectives. The most common tools or methodologies used in the execution stage include Risk Analysis, Balanced Scorecards, Business Plan Review, and Milestone Assessment.

Project Closure

In the closure stage, the project is phased-out or formally terminated. The closure process is often gradual as the project is weaned of resources and personnel are reallocated to other organizational needs. Acceptance of deliverables is an important part of project closure. The closure phase is characterized by a written formal project review report containing the following components: a formal acceptance of the final product, Weighted Critical Measurements (matching the initial requirements with the final product delivered), rewarding the team, a list of lessons learned, releasing project resources, and a formal project closure notification to management and other stakeholders. A common tool for project closure is Project Closure Report.

Hierarchy of Project Framework

The project life cycle involves several dimensions, which must all be coordinated within a hierarchical structure covering the levels below:

1. System level (e.g., University system within which an institution resides)
2. Program level (e.g., Specific academic programs within an institution)
3. Project level (e.g., Cycle-based curriculum endeavors, such as pursuit of accreditation)
4. Task level (e.g., Preparation of self-assessment report)
5. Activity level (e.g., Documentation of specific course folders for review purposes)

For a personal project, most of the project management efforts will be focused at the task and activity levels, assuming that leadership support and enabling environment are already in place. A key requirement for a successful project is to ensure that all appropriate functional linkages are in place. Using a project framework in any endeavor has the following advantages:

1. A project framework is documented such that other project teams could replicate the template for other efforts.
2. A project framework that has been proven for corporate projects can be adopted for personal undertakings.

3. A project framework ensures that critical and logical steps in a project effort are not neglected.

Global Applications of Project Management

Project management has worldwide application. It is a common language of getting things done in every corner of the world, ranging from primitive villages to much advanced society. Project management can help you not to miss the boat, so to speak, as depicted in Figure 2.3. Project management is applicable to all human endeavors; ranging from transportation, home management, job search, shopping, cooking, construction, manufacturing, education, neighborhood watch, delivery, health care, remodeling, public service, customer service, sales, and so on.

Has the ship sailed off yet?

Figure 2.3: Transportation application of Project Management

Whatever it is, we can get it done through project management. Project management skills are needed and highly valued at all corners of the world. So prevalent is this realization that the Project Management Institute has an envisioned goal that is summarized below. Figure 2.4 illustrates the global reaches of project management.

"worldwide, organizations will embrace, value, and utilize project management and attribute their success to it."

Figure 2.4: Global Project Management

Practical Project Management

In everything you do, think "project." This book is designed to be a personal and practical resource for hands-on project management, using interactive and iterative approaches to stimulate interests in applying project management techniques to everyday challenges. The book constitutes a *street-wise* presentation of proven corporate approaches to managing projects. By using logical task selection and activity sequencing, you can get more done within time and cost constraints. The levels of getting things done can be put into the following categories:

- Things that are done for personal objectives (home projects)
- Things that are done at departmental task level (team work)
- Things that are done at enterprise level (organizational tasks)

Everyone belongs somewhere along the above functional axes,

and project Management proficiency is needed at each level. The categories for applying project management include the following:

- Personal projects
- Organizational projects
- Professional projects

Just as in the corporate environment, every project faces three primary constraints of:

- Schedule (expressed in time limitations)
- Budget (expressed in cost restrictions)
- Scope (expressed in performance and quality expectations)

Project objectives are achieved through trade-offs among competing requirements of time, cost, and scope. Figure 2.5 shows the trade-offs axes. The bottom line of project management revolves around a disciplined approach to getting things done. If you manage the three constraints above effectively, using personal trade-offs, you will get more done in the long run. You should weigh the effectiveness of how things are done versus the efficiency with which they are done.

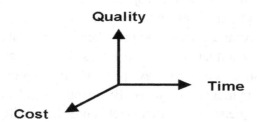

Figure 2.5: Trade-off axes for Time, Cost, and Quality

The most effective way to perform a task is not necessarily the most efficient way. One may be effective in getting something done, but may be very inefficient in doing so.

Effectiveness is the ability to accomplish a desired result. For example, driving several miles to hand-deliver a message certainly gets the message there. But the same message might be better delivered through alternate means, such as a telephone call or fax.

Efficiency is the accomplishment of output with respect to expenditure of resource inputs. That is, efficiency measures the ratio of output to input.

Juggle Multiple Projects

Things to do often come "in bunches," otherwise known as projects. Rarely would tasks come in a serial sequence. They must be juggled as depicted by the caricature in Figure 2.6. We are all familiar with the usual demand of multi-tasking. Most of us do that very well. But things that we do through multi-tasking often include many activities that do not hold much value for our overall goals. Multi-tasking is sensible only if the multiple tasks are essential and value-adding. Many people are not good at separating the wheat from the chaff. That means we falter at distinguishing value-adding activities from valueless engagements. In order to succeed with our personal and professional goals, we must learn to juggle multiple activities, literally, without dropping the figurative ball. This requires prioritization and learning to determine which activities can be run concurrently without excessive physical overload. Common examples are summarized below: Run washing machine while cooking. Cooking requires full and direct attention, whereas, once loaded, a washing machine requires little or no attention until its change of cycle occurs.

Figure 2.6: Juggler of Multiple Projects

You can get more done by reducing the size of what you have to do. When you have "a lot on your plate," you must develop a plan to either reduce the size of your plate or make sure not much get on the plate you've got.

Don't Drop the Ball

Be mindful of where and how you drop the ball in your project management endeavors. Planning is a pre-requisite to everything.

Logical scheduling of activities is essential. Control is necessary. To execute all of these aspects of project management requires self-discipline and personal control. Self-control that is exercised in many aspects of our lives also moves on to serve other project goals positively. Personal discipline in such aspects as spending cautiously, saving dedicatedly, careful selection of social relationships, discernment in entertainment choices, shunning of reckless talk, avoidance of stressful thoughts, and perseverance toward healthy living all contribute to how we can dedicate ourselves to value-adding activities. In discernment of actions, we should learn to say "no" to things that we really don't want. We should avoid making too many commitments, particularly those that create conflicts of time, budget, and work performance. Stressful thoughts consume time and detract from value-adding pursuits.

Work hard to avoid "dropping the ball" in planning, scheduling, controlling, and closing out tasks. Figure 2.7 illustrates this point cogently. Planning is the map of the wise. Develop a plan and stick to it, either in its original form or in a modified form based on prevailing circumstances.

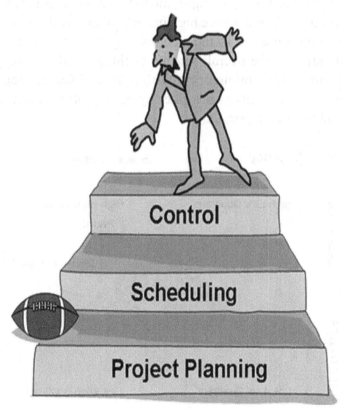

Figure 2-7: Don't Drop the Ball while Climbing Project Steps

Manage Priorities

"The urgent problems are seldom the important ones."

- President Dwight D. Eisenhower

When multi-tasking, we must evaluate what should have priority. An assessment of what is important versus what is urgent will help identify priority items. Not all tasks can be of equal "high" priority. What is important is not necessarily urgent; and what we often perceive as urgent is not really important. Figure 2.8 shows the trade-offs between what is important and what is urgent. Tasks that are important and urgent have high priority. Those with low urgency and low importance fall in the "ignore" region; and do not deserve much attention in the overall scheme of things. Unfortunately, our lives are often ruled by urgency. With proper project management techniques, we can manage priorities by trading-off between what is urgent and what is important.

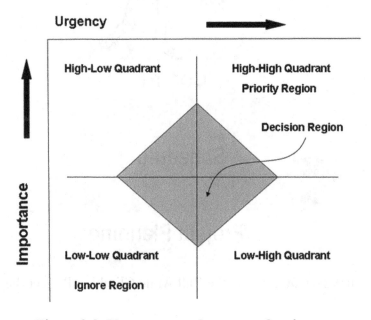

Figure 2.8: Urgent versus Important Quadrants

Manage Risks

As the saying goes, "you cannot accumulate if you don't speculate." Taking risk is part of getting things done. But the risk must be weighed against the prevailing cost and the opportunity to advance quality. The graphics in Figure 2-9 illustrate the importance of risk, quality, time, and cost.

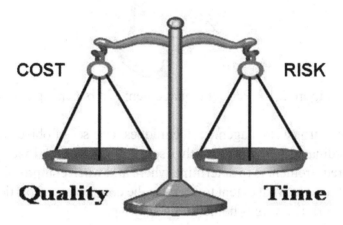

Figure 2-9: Weighing Cost, Risk, Quality and Time Factors

Balance Work and Play

"Life is like riding a bicycle. In order to keep your balance, you must keep moving."

- Albert Einstein

Like the bike rider in Figure 2.10, one must balance projects through work and play. You must keep your feet properly planted on the tasks that matter and avoid falling over the edge of the steps of project management. In project management, one must deal with multiple objectives that often compete for time and resources. This is particularly critical when balancing regular work objectives with irregular personal objectives.

Figure 2.10: Project management is a balancing act

By using project management techniques, one set of objectives can be coordinated to support another set of objectives, and vice versa. A key requirement is to determine where and when compromises are possible and to what extent to exercise the compromises; particularly where work life versus home life is an issue.

Work Life versus Home Life

Professional, Corporate, Family, Friends, Neighbors

Haste makes Waste

Take time to get things done right the first time. Haste makes waste and leads to non-value-adding corrective actions later on. You are your own best advocate. Humans have morbid fascination with other's failure, tragedy, and accidents. Don't allow your project to create a spectacle for rubber-necking onlookers.

Learn from Mistakes

"You must learn from the mistakes of others. You can't possibly live long enough to make them all yourself."

- Sam Levenson (1911 - 1980)

Mistakes are essential for learning and learning is essential for future project success. Plan what you need to do. Execute as planned. Learn from the project and document lessons learned. It is essential to close out a task. Closing a project is as important as initiating it. Not closing a task promptly often leads to project failure. Use the close-out to plan and initiate the next project. This process is summarized in the PELC (Plan-Execute-Learn-Close) quadrants of project success that is shown in Figure 2.11.

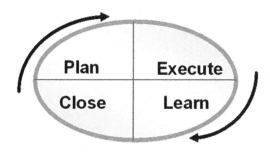

Figure 2.11: Plan-Execute-Learn-Close Loop Quadrants

While preparing for mistakes, we must also take precautions. As it is often said, **"measure twice and cut once."** Precautions that are taken to preempt errors result in saving time. Time, thus saved, can be redirected at more productive activities. Resources are scarce and we should not engage in wasteful mistakes.

Watch out for Octopus Projects

Octopus projects are those projects that spread their "tentacles" to the far reaches of an organization. They become operational cancers that are difficult to eradicate. They creep into every facet of the organization without providing justification for their continuation and without any value-adding basis. If these "Octopusical" projects are not closed, they continue to consume time and resources while detracting from valuable accomplishments.

Chapter Three

Streamlining and Simplifying Work

Haste makes waste just as rush makes crash.

Getting more things done requires focusing on fewer things to do.

Never spend time and effort on an activity that has little or no potential for providing value or generating a benefit.

This implies that we must "separate the wheat from the chaff," when deciding on what needs to be done. We must be able to distinguish value-adding activities from wasteful activities. That means, we must operate "lean" and cut out non-value-adding activities. Figure 3.1 is a Pareto Distribution showing that only about 20% of what we do is actually value-adding. As much as 80% of our activities could be going into wasteful engagements.

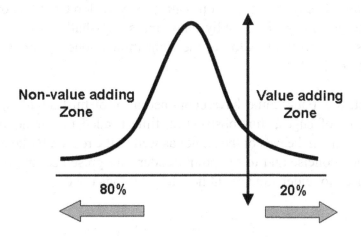

Figure 3.1: Pareto Distribution of Activities

Studies have shown that trying to do too much often leads to getting less done. Tackling too much makes the "doer" more error prone, thereby leading to rework and subsequent waste of corrective time.

The Pareto distribution is often extended to what is called ABC analysis, whereby items are organized into A, B, and C categories. These can be explained as follows:

A Category: Top 10% in order of value (absolutely essential).

B Category: Middle 80% in order of value (essential).

C Category: Bottom 10% in order of value (non-essential).

The C Category is often a "lost cause" and can be eliminated without much adverse consequence. By eliminating this, you will have more time to focus on the essential items. You will, consequently, be getting more done by focusing on fewer essential items.

Simplification helps to get more things done

Too often in life, we allow inconsequential lifestyles activities to rob us of time to get *really* valuable things done. You cannot hem-and-haw all day and then complain that you don't have enough time to get things done. Dilly-dally and shilly-shally ways of life rob us of opportunities to get the right things done promptly and satisfactorily.

In fact, this book could have contained a lot of fluff stretching to hundreds of pages, thus obstructing time needed to pursue other things both on the part of the author as well as the reader. By keeping the book concise and to the point, readers are presented only what they need to understand about how to get things done.

First Principle

The author proposes the first principle of getting things done. This is referred to as Badiru's first principle:

"To get more done, try and do less."

There are little nagging things that consume time every day. They are usually of little or no value. Eliminate them and you will have more discretionary time to yourself. Saving time through project management gives you time to do other things that you really want to do.

If Albert Einstein had attempted to do several things in the years that he was fiddling with his theory of relativity, he probably would not have gotten it done when he did. Leonardo da Vinci (of the Mona Lisa fame) was reputed to not have been a good project manager because he died with several unfinished projects in various stages of incompleteness. What would have happened if he had focused on a few projects that were actually finished?

In order to get more done, you need to be more selective with social impositions. Such impositions create more things to do and less time to do the most crucial tasks. You don't have to visit Joe and Jane every time they issue an invitation for a gathering. You don't really have to attend every social function for which you have an invitation, no matter how sumptuous the Hors D'oeuvres might be. Identify what not to do at all. Identify what to do and in what order. Set goals and hold firm to the goals. Flip-flopping between setting goals and dismantling them with inaction does not leave room for actually getting things done.

Common Laws of Project Management

There are several guiding principles for project management. These are presented here as common laws of project management. They serve as philosophical and practical guidelines.

Parkinson's Law:

"Work expands to fill the available time."
Translation:- Idle time in project schedule creates opportunity for ineffective utilization of time.

Badiru's Theory:

"Grass is always greener where you most need it to be dead."
Translation:- Problems fester naturally if left alone. Control must be exercised in order to preempt problems. Don't concede to others what you can control yourself.

Peter's Principle:

"People rise to the level of their incompetence."
Translation:- Get the right person into the right job.

Murphy's Law:

"Whatever can go wrong will."
Translation:- Project planning must make allowance for contingencies.

Axiom of Starting Early

"Early to bed and early to rise makes a man healthy, wealthy, and wise."

- Benjamin Franklin

Get started promptly with whatever needs to be done. What is worth doing is worth doing at the earliest opportunity. The old adage of "early to bed, early to rise" is very applicable to managing projects effectively and getting things done. The best things in life are done early in the morning. Milking cow is a good example. By contrast, most evils occur at night. The occurrence of crime is a good example.

Farmers happily embrace the "early start" adage; and that is why this author loves farmers. The USA Army used to advertise that they "get more done before 9a.m. than most people get done all day." That is, indeed, the truth; and that is why this author loves the military. It is sad that the old adage of starting early has been replaced by the new truism of putting things off as late as possible. It is hoped that the lessons provided in this book will encourage readers to recapture the essence of what got our forefathers to the exalted level of work ethics that they handed down to us.

Chapter Four

Applying Project Management

Get it done and put it behind you.

━━━━━━━━━━━━━━━━━━━━━━━━━━━━━

In this book, the author brings the proven tools and techniques of project management from the corporate world to the pedestrian level for practical street-wise application to both personal and professional projects. The book is designed as a self-help resource and self-paced guide for everyone.

Once the set of activities to be performed have been determined and pruned, the value-adding activities that remain must be managed in accordance with the tools and techniques of project management.

In business applications, a project is defined as a temporary endeavor undertaken to create a unique product, service, or result. Most typical projects are undertaken for the purpose of creating a product. But, realistically, human efforts generate all types of outputs, which may fall in any of the following three major categories of outputs:

1. Physical products (e.g., consumer products)
2. Service results (e.g., business function to serve customers)
3. Results (e.g., training outcome).

Most projects fall under five major phases as listed below:

1. Planning
2. Organizing
3. Scheduling
4. Monitoring and Control
5. Phase-out

But these are very broad phases. Thus, they are often expanded to include more details of what goes into each of the general phases. Depending on the application and the level of detail desired, a project may be divided into up six or more phases. In general, project management is the application of knowledge, skills, tools and techniques to project activities to meet project requirements. In most corporate applications, project management is accomplished through the application of six major steps, which comprise the project management process as discussed earlier in Chapter 2 and summarized below:

1. Initiating
2. Planning
3. Executing
4. Monitoring
5. Controlling
6. Closing

Specific strategic, operational, and tactical goals and objectives are embedded within each step of a project. For example, "initiating" may consist of project conceptualization and description. Part of "executing" may include resource allocation and scheduling. "Monitoring" may involve project tracking, data collection, and parameter measurement. "Controlling" implies taking corrective action based on the items that are monitored and evaluated. "Closing" involves phasing out or terminating a project. Closing does not necessarily mean a death sentence for a project; as the end of one project may be used as the stepping stone to the next series of endeavors. The entire project lifecycle involves integration and coordination of People and Process under the influence of "Project Politics" known as the PPP effect shown in Figure 4.1. The fact is that the larger the number of people involved in an endeavor, the more politics will come into play; and we have to recognize and be adept at handling and resolving it.

Figure 4.1: Interface of People, Process, and Project Politics

The initiation of a project can be likened to the take-off of a plane on a journey of goals and objectives. The closing of the project is similar to the landing of the plane. As in any normal plane trip, the landing of the plane represents the beginning of the next journey --- a road trip to the final destination. So, the closing of one project simply serves as the beginning (initiation) of the next endeavor. With this re-assurance, the typical fear and apprehension of closing a project can be allayed.

In executing a project, working hard is not the only option. Working smart provides better long-term benefits. The author often uses the analogy of a novice swimmer. The novice swimmer works the hardest, huffing and puffing, but with very little distance covered. By contrast, an expert swimmer covers more distance with very little effort. So, an observation of "hard work" does not necessarily imply work progress. The SMART notion of project objectives is expanded below:

Specific: Project objectives must be specific, explicit, and unambiguous. Objectives that are not specific are subject to misinterpretations and misuse.

Measurable: Project objectives should be designed to be measurable. Any factor that cannot be measured cannot be tracked, evaluated, or controlled. Strategic planning requires measurable near-term objectives to ensure that things are done well.

Aligned: A project's goals and objectives must be aligned with the core strategy of an organization and relevant to prevailing needs. If not aligned, an objective will have misplaced impacts. The alignment of strategy and task performance creates agility.

Realistic: A project and its essential elements must be realistic and achievable. It is good to "dream" and have lofty ideas of what can be achieved. But if those pursuits are not realistic, a project will just end up "spinning wheels" without any significant achievements.

Timed: Timing is the standardized basis for work accomplishment. If project expectations are not normalized against time, there would be no basis for accurate assessment of performance. Timed responsiveness makes it possible to adapt to a continually changing environment.

Put simply, project management is the process of getting things done. Everybody needs project management. From large corporations to government institutes, project management ranks high as organizational asset to optimize operations.

Every Endeavor is a Project

If you want results, use project management. Every endeavor can be defined as a project, consisting of a set of activities that are choreographed toward an identifiable goal. A project can be simple (e.g., painting a vacant room) or very complex (e.g., launching a satellite). Even simple personal projects can become complicated enough to warrant the application of formal project management approaches. Every individual wants more results in less time at lower cost. It is through the structured approach of project management that we can logically trade-off between competing objectives. The application of project management is vital in business, industry, government, and personal activities. Everyone and every organization needs project management because projects offer an avenue for the accomplishment of human effort. The core competencies that employers often require of new employees include *leadership*, *team skills*, and *project management*.

So often is project management required in an organization that most now use Management-By-Projects (MBP) as a primary business strategy. MBP has several benefits. It helps the process of learning leadership practices, team building, employee relations, interpersonal skills, and communication skills. Most projects have the same things in common:

- Productivity of Workers (Performance)

- Resource Shortage (Budget)

- Time Constraint (Schedule)

Project principles, similarities, and practices are transferable across industries, across cultures, and across geographical boundaries; and are applicable to personal projects. This makes MBP very versatile and generally applicable to different organization sizes, shapes, and locations.

Project organizing involves selecting an organizational structure for the project and categorizing the players and stakeholders in the project. The personal and individual needs of those involved in a project must be taken into account. Maslow's Hierarchy of Needs, summarized below, provides guidance to recognizing people's needs at different levels:

1. **Physiological Needs:** The needs for the basic necessities of life, such as food, water, housing, and clothing (Survival

Needs). This is the level where access to wages is most critical. The basic needs are of primary concern in many developing economies.

2. **Safety Need:** The needs for security, stability, and freedom from threat of physical harm.

3. **Social Needs:** The needs for social approval, friends, love, affection, and association. For example, project outsourcing may bring about better economic outlook that may enable each individual to be in a better position to meet his or her social needs.

4. **Esteem Needs:** The needs for accomplishment, respect, recognition, attention, and appreciation. These needs are important not only at the individual level, but also at the organizational level.

5. **Self-Actualization Needs:** These are the needs for self-fulfillment and self-improvement. They also involve the stage of opportunity to grow professionally. Project outsourcing may create opportunities for individuals to assert themselves socially and economically.

Project Outline

The outline below provides a guide for determining the key elements that go into managing any type and level of a project. The outline can be expanded or collapsed to fit the specific needs and prevailing circumstances of any project. Not all the line items in this template will be applicable or logical for some projects.

1. Planning

    I.   Specify Project Background
        a. Define current situation and process
            1. Understand the process

2. Identify important variables
3. Quantify variables
    b. Identify areas for improvement
      1. List and explain areas
      2. Study potential strategy for solution

II.   Define unique terminologies relevant to the project
      1. Industry-specific terminologies
      2. Company-specific terminologies
      3. Project-specific terminologies

III.   Define Project goal and objectives
    a. Write a mission statement
    b. Solicit inputs and ideas from personnel
    c. Develop Statement of Work (SOW)

IV.   Establish performance standards
    a. Schedule
    b. Performance
    c. Cost

V.   Conduct formal project feasibility
    a. Determine impact on cost
    b. Determine impact on organization
    c. Determine project deliverables

VI.   Secure management Support

2. Organizing

I.   Identify project-management team
    a. Specify project-organization structure
      1. Matrix structure
      2. Formal and informal structures
      3. Justify structure
    b. Specify departments to be involved and key personnel
      1. Purchasing

2. Materials management

3. Engineering, design, manufacturing, etc.

   c. Define project-management responsibilities

1. Select project manager

2. Write project charter

3. Establish project policies and procedures

  II.   Implement Triple C Model

    a. Communication

1. Identify communication interfaces

2. Use a communication Matrix

    b. Cooperation

1. Outline cooperation requirements

    c. Coordination

1. Develop work-breakdown structure

2. Assign task responsibilities

3. Develop responsibility chart

3. Scheduling and Resource Allocation

  I.   Develop master schedule

    a. Estimate task duration

    b. Identify task-precedence requirements

1. Technical precedence

2. Resource-imposed precedence

3. Procedural precedence

    c. Use common project management tools

1. CPM

2. PERT

3. Gantt chart

4. Tracking, Reporting, and Control

  I.   Establish guidelines for tracking, reporting, and control

    a. Define data requirement

1. Data categories

2. Data characterization

3. Measurement scales
   b. Develop data documentation
      1. Data-update requirements
      2. Data-quality control
      3. Establish data-security measures

II.   Categorize control points
   a. Schedule audit
      1. Activity network and Gantt charts
      2. Milestones
      3. Delivery schedule
   b. Performance audit
      1. Employee performance
      2. Product quality
   c. Cost audit
      1. Cost-containment measures
      2. Percent completion versus budget depletion

III. Identify and implement control actions

IV.   Phase-out the project
   a. Performance review
   b. Strategy for follow-up projects
   c. Personnel retention and releases

V.   Document project and submit final report

The summary lesson from this book is that taking on more than you can chew within the available time, will only lead to effort failures, disappointments, and frustration. We should always use an incremental approach to accomplish each stage and milestone toward the final goal. Yes, you can be "Jack of 'best' trades," picking only the best efforts to attempt. Yes, you can be a self-actuating project manager to get things done at the level you never thought possible. Project management makes this to be possible and to become a reality.

Project Charter

In the business world, a project charter is used to give notice of a project. The project charter is primarily an announcement of the project and all its ramifications. It establishes the project manager's right to make decisions about how the project will be executed. As a formal document (as caricatured in Figure 4.2), the project charter summarizes the requirements, management, and financial aspects of a project. It outlines the scope, objectives, benefits, costs, and those involved in the project. Although, one would not need to develop a formal charter for personal projects, it helps to have an understanding of what a charter entails and use that understanding to guide decisions pertaining to personal projects. If nothing else, a conceptualization of the project charter creates an awareness of who is involved and who will be impacted by specific actions that we take in personal day-to-day decisions and activities.

Figure 4.2: Written Documentation of Project Charter

In organizational projects, the purpose of a project charter is to empower the project team and demonstrate management support for the project and the project manager. A charter can also be used by the sponsor to provide general direction for the project and delineate requirements. The charter normally precedes other project documents. It establishes the project manager's authority for the project. Stakeholder agreements are also often based on the contents of the project charter. It is important to do the following when developing or contemplating project charters:

- Recognize key elements of a project charter
- Understand the use of a charter
- Appreciate the benefits and requirements of developing a charter

In summary, a project charter has the following benefits:

- Clarifying business goals
- Defining objectives and scope
- Getting buy-in from stakeholders
- Devising a strategy for managing the project
- Establishing team roles and responsibilities
- Establishing a timeline
- Identifying required resources
- Identifying potential risks

Primary elements of a project charter include:

- Purpose
- Scope
- Goals
- Plan

Define Purpose of the Project

What is your Purpose?

Can you make a business or personal case for your project?

Is there a need for the project?

Can you clearly explain the need for the project in a few words?

Where does it fall relative to your other projects and goals?

Specify Scope of the Project

- Identify what you and your team will focus on for the project:
    o Task Analysis
    o Work Design
    o Redesign of Requirements
    o Tool and Technology Usage
- Focus on what is important
- Establish limits so that the project is manageable
- Keep the project aligned with expectations and available resources
- Be specific --- The more specific the better!!
- Get approval and buy-in from those to be involved (colleagues, family, friends, team members, and so on)

Establish Goals of the Project

- What are your targets?
- How much variability is acceptable?
- How much risk is reasonable?
- Can you measure your effectiveness?
- When do you plan on achieving the goals?

Develop a Plan for the Project

- Outline Project Elements and Milestones
    o List all major activities
    o Estimate duration from start to end
    o Identify resources
    o Identify deliverables

- Implement the plan
    o Measure progress and identify corrective actions
    o Show and maintain direction
    o Justify resources
    o Communicate to shareholders
    o Ensure you stay on time and on budget

o Ensure results
o Periodically reinforce buy-in

- **Utilize Sources of Information**
  o Listen to the voice of your constituents or clients. Examples are:
    o Voice Of Client (VOC)
    o Voice Of Associates (VOA)
    o Voice of Family (VOF)
  o Transform client requirements into objective measures.
  o Perform a gap analyses of where deficiencies exist.
  o Assess the risk of not meeting goals and the risk of undertaking the project.

- **Use Project Charter Effectively**
  o A project charter can be very effective for managing a project.
  o Use project charter to provide focus on what is important and when things need to be completed.
  o Avoid spending too much time finalizing the charter. It is a living document and subject to revision as the project progresses.
  o Periodically revisit and update the charter.

Overcome Administrative Impediment

There is never a perfect time to get things done . . . if we waited for the perfect time, we would never get anything done. It is important to overcome administrative impediments, which often prevent or retard project success. Total project success requires that all functions operation at their respective peak performance levels. The light-hearted satire below, which has been circulating widely on The Internet, typifies the reality of the impediments that dysfunctional management processes can create in any project.

"New Element Discovered"

- Author unknown

"The heaviest element known to science was discovered recently by physicists at the Worldwide Research Lab in Amsterdam, The Netherlands. The element, tentatively named "Administratium." has no protons or electrons and thus has an atomic number of 0. However, it does have 1 neutron, 125 assistant neutrons, 75 vice neutrons, and 111 assistant vice neutrons. This gives it an atomic mass of 312. These 312 particles are held together in a nucleus by a force that involves the continuous exchange of meson-like particles called morons.

Since it has no electrons, Administratium is inert. However, it can be detected chemically as it impedes every reaction it comes in contact with. According to the discoverers, a minute amount of Administratium caused one reaction to take over four days to complete, when it would normally occur in less than one second.

Administratium has a normal half-life of approximately 3 years, at which time it does not actually decay, but instead, undergoes a reorganization in which assistant neutrons, vice neutrons, and assistant vice neutrons change places. Some studies have shown that the atomic weight actually increases after each reorganization.

Research at other laboratories indicates that Administratium occurs naturally in the atmosphere. It tends to concentrate at certain points such as government agencies, large corporations, universities, and most organizations who employ more than 10 people. It can actually be found in the newest, best maintained buildings.

Scientists point out that Administratium is known to be toxic at any level of concentration and can easily destroy any positive reactions where it is allowed to accumulate. Attempts are being made to determine how Administratium can be controlled to prevent irreversible damage, but results to date are not promising."

To overcome administrative implements, do the following:

- Use project management to plan, organize, and control projects.
- Use tools and techniques of project management to coordinate efforts.
- Identify project goals and scope the project around the goals.
- Use the right tool for the right job.
- Fit the right person to the right function.
- Achieve operational efficiencies in administrative processes by weeding out non-value-adding steps.
- Phase-out projects promptly once the desired goals have been accomplished.

Chapter Five

Work Breakdown Structure

"Divide-and-conquer" works for getting things done

Work Breakdown Structure (WBS) refers to the itemization of a project for planning, scheduling, and control purposes. The eventual goal is specified at the top of the WBS diagram, which may also be viewed as the Project Outline. It presents the inherent components of a project in a structured block diagram or interrelationship flow chart. WBS shows the relative hierarchies of parts (phases, segments, milestone, etc.) of the project. The purpose of constructing a WBS is to analyze the elemental components of the project in detail. If a project is properly designed through the application of WBS at the project planning stage, it becomes easier to estimate cost and time requirements of the project. Project control is also enhanced by the ability to identify how components of the project link together. Tasks that are contained in the WBS collectively describe the overall project goal. Figure 5.1 illustrates how the project goal sits atop the waves of tasks making up a project.

Overall project planning and control can be improved by using a WBS approach. A large project may be broken down into smaller sub-projects that may, in turn, be systematically broken down into task groups. Thus, WBS permits the implementation of a "divide and conquer" concept for project control. An example of a WBS layout is shown in Figure 5.2.

Figure 5.1: Dominance of Project Goal

In the WBS design, the overall goal is at the top of the structure, followed by all the sub-elements that lead up to the goal. Individual components in a WBS are referred to as WBS elements, and the hierarchy of each is designated by a Level identifier. Elements at the same level of subdivision are said to be of the same WBS level. Descending levels provide increasingly detailed definition of project tasks. The complexity of a project and the degree of control desired determine the number of levels in the WBS. Each component is successively broken down into smaller details at lower levels. The process may continue until specific project activities are noted on the WBS diagram.

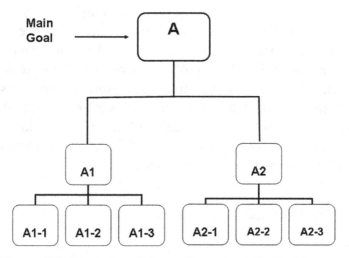

Figure 5.2: Work Breakdown Structure (WBS) Diagram

In effect, the structure of the WBS looks very much like an organizational chart. The basic approach for preparing a WBS is as follows:

Level 1 WBS

This contains only the final goal of the project. This item should be identifiable directly as an organizational budget item.

Level 2 WBS

This level contains the major sub-sections of the project. These sub-sections are usually identified by their contiguous location or by their related purposes.

Level 3 WBS

Level 3 of the WBS structure contains definable components of the level 2 sub-sections. In technical terms, this may be referred to as the finite element level of the project.

Subsequent levels of WBS are constructed in more specific details depending on the span of control desired. If a complete WBS becomes too crowded, separate WBS layouts may be drawn for the Level 2 components. A statement of work (SOW) or WBS summary should accompany the WBS. The SOW is a narrative of the work to be done. It should include the objectives of the work, its scope, resource requirements, tentative due date, feasibility statements, and so on. A good analysis of the WBS structure will make it easier to perform resource requirement analysis. Figure 5.3 shows the hierarchical relationships between levels of a project.

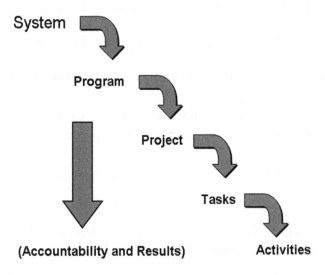

Figure 5.3: Hierarchy of Project Levels

Project Organization Chart

Along with work breakdown structure and project planning, a project organization chart must be developed. Even if not drawn out graphically, the chart must be developed, at least conceptually, to show where each person or group belongs in the project structure. There are many alternate forms of project organization chart. Before selecting an organizational structure, the project team should assess the nature of the job to be performed and its requirements.

The organization structure may be defined in terms of functional

54

specializations, departmental proximity, standard management boundaries, operational relationships, or product requirements. In personal projects, the organization structure may be informal and selected based on convenience. It is important to communicate the organization chart to all those involved in the project as depicted in Figure 5.4.

Figure 5.4: Communicating the Organization Chart

Traditional Formal Organization Structures

Many organizations use the traditional formal or classical organization structures, which show hierarchical relationships between individuals or teams of individuals. Traditional formal organizational structures are effective in service enterprises because groups with similar functional responsibilities are clustered at the same level of the structure. A formal organizational structure represents the officially sanctioned structure of a functional area. An informal organizational structure, on the other hand, develops when people organize themselves in an unofficial way to accomplish a project objective. The informal organization is often very subtle in that not everyone in the organization is aware of its existence. Both formal and informal organizations exist within every project. Positive characteristics of the traditional formal organizational structure include the following:

- Availability of broad manpower base
- Identifiable technical line of control
- Grouping of specialists to share technical knowledge
- Collective line of responsibility
- Possibility of assigning personnel to several different projects
- Clear hierarchy for supervision
- Continuity and consistency of functional disciplines
- Possibility for the establishment of departmental policies, procedures, and missions.

However, the traditional formal structure does have some negative characteristics as summarized below:

- No one individual is directly responsible for the total project
- Project-oriented planning may be impeded
- There may not be a clear line of reporting up from the lower levels
- Coordination is complex
- A higher level of cooperation is required between adjacent levels
- The strongest functional group may wrongfully claim project authority.

Functional Organization

The most common type of formal organization is known as the functional organization, whereby people are organized into groups dedicated to particular functions. Depending on the size and the type of auxiliary activities involved, several minor, but supporting, functional units can be developed for a project. Projects that are organized along functional lines normally reside in a specific department or area of specialization. The project home office or headquarters is located in the specific functional department. The advantages of a functional organization structure are presented below:

- Improved accountability
- Discernible lines of control
- Flexibility in manpower utilization
- Enhanced comradeship of technical staff
- Improved productivity of specially skilled personnel
- Potential for staff advancement along functional path
- Ability of the home office to serve as a refuge for project problems.

The disadvantages of a functional organization structure include:

- Potential division of attention between project goals and regular functions
- Conflict between project objectives and regular functions
- Poor coordination of similar project responsibilities
- Unreceptive attitudes on the part of the surrogate department
- Multiple layers of management
- Lack of concentrated effort.

Product Organization

Another approach to organizing a project is to use the end product or goal of the project as the determining factor for personnel structure. This is often referred to as pure project organization or simply project organization. The project is set up as a unique entity within the parent organization. It has its own dedicated technical staff and administration. It is linked to the rest of the system through progress reports, organizational policies, procedures, and funding. The interface between product-organized projects and other elements of the organization may be strict or liberal, depending on the organization.

The product organization is common in industries that have multiple product lines. Unlike the functional, the product organization decentralizes functions. It creates a unit consisting of specialized skills around a given project or product. Sometimes referred to as a team, task force, or product group, the product organization is common in public, research, and manufacturing organizations where specially organized and designated groups are assigned specific functions. A major advantage of the product organization is that it gives the project members a feeling of dedication to and identification with a particular goal.

A possible shortcoming of the product organization is the requirement that the product group be sufficiently funded to be able to stand alone. The product group may be viewed as an ad hoc unit that is formed for the purpose of a specific goal. The personnel involved in the project are dedicated to the particular mission at hand. At the conclusion of the mission, they may be reassigned to other projects. Product organization can facilitate the most diverse and flexible grouping of project participants. It has the following advantages:

- Simplicity of structure
- Unity of project purpose
- Localization of project failures
- Condensed and focused communication lines
- Full authority of the project manager
- Quicker decisions due to centralized authority
- Skill development due to project specialization
- Improved motivation, commitment, and concentration
- Flexibility in determining time, cost, performance trade-offs
- Project team's reporting directly to one project manager or boss
- Ability of individuals to acquire and maintain expertise on a given project.

The disadvantages of product organization are:

- Narrow view on the part of project personnel (as opposed to a global organizational view)

- Mutually exclusive allocation of resources (one worker to one project)
- Duplication of efforts on different but similar projects
- Monopoly of organizational resources
- Worker concern about life after the project
- Reduced skill diversification.

One other disadvantage of the product organization is the difficulty supervisors have in assessing the technical competence of individual team members. Since managers are leading people in fields foreign to them, it is difficult for them to assess technical capability. Many major organizations have this problem. Those who can talk a good game and give good presentations are often viewed by management as knowledgeable, regardless of their true technical capabilities.

Matrix Organization Structure

The matrix organization is a frequently-used organization structure in industry. It is used where there is multiple managerial accountability and responsibility for a project. It combines the advantages of the traditional structure and the product organization structure. The hybrid configuration of the matrix structure facilitates maximum resource utilization and increased performance within time, cost, and performance constraints. There are usually two chains of command involving both horizontal and vertical reporting lines. The horizontal line deals with the functional line of responsibility while the vertical line deals with the project line of responsibility.

Advantages of matrix organization include the following:

- Good team interaction
- Consolidation of objectives
- Multilateral flow of information
- Lateral mobility for job advancement
- Individuals have an opportunity to work on a variety of projects
- Efficient sharing and utilization of resources

- Reduced project cost due to sharing of personnel
- Continuity of functions after project completion
- Stimulating interactions with other functional teams
- Functional lines rally to support the project efforts
- Each person has a "home" office after project completion
- Company knowledge base is equally available to all projects.

Some of the disadvantages of matrix organization are summarized below:

- Matrix response time may be slow for fast-paced projects
- Each project organization operates independently
- Overhead cost due to additional lines of command
- Potential conflict of project priorities
- Problems inherent in having multiple bosses
- Complexity of the structure.

Traditionally, industrial projects are conducted in serial functional implementations such as R&D, engineering, manufacturing, and marketing. At each stage, unique specifications and work patterns may be used without consulting the preceding and succeeding phases. The consequence is that the end product may not possess the original intended characteristics. For example, the first project in the series might involve the production of one component while the subsequent projects might involve the production of other components. The composite product may not achieve the desired performance because the components were not designed and produced from a unified point of view. The major appeal of matrix organization is that it attempts to provide synergy within groups in an organization.

Project Feasibility Analysis

The feasibility of a project can be ascertained in terms of technical factors, economic factors, or both. A feasibility study is documented with a report showing all the ramifications of the project and should be broken down into the following categories.

Technical feasibility: "Technical feasibility" refers to the ability of the process to take advantage of the current state of the technology in pursuing further improvement. The technical capability of the personnel as well as the capability of the available technology should be considered.

Managerial feasibility: Managerial feasibility involves the capability of the infrastructure of a process to achieve and sustain process improvement. Management support, employee involvement, and commitment are key elements required to ascertain managerial feasibility.

Economic feasibility: This involves the ability of the proposed project to generate economic benefits. A benefit-cost analysis and a breakeven analysis are important aspects of evaluating the economic feasibility of new projects. The tangible and intangible aspects of a project should be translated into economic terms to facilitate a consistent basis for evaluation.

Financial feasibility: Financial feasibility should be distinguished from economic feasibility. Financial feasibility involves the capability of the project organization to raise the appropriate funds needed to implement the proposed project. Project financing can be a major obstacle in large multi-party projects because of the level of capital required. Loan availability, credit worthiness, equity, and loan schedule are important aspects of financial feasibility analysis.

Cultural feasibility: Cultural feasibility deals with the compatibility of the proposed project with the cultural setup of the project environment. In labor-intensive projects, planned functions must be integrated with the local cultural practices and beliefs. For example, religious beliefs may influence what an individual is willing to do or not do.

Social feasibility: Social feasibility addresses the influences that a proposed project may have on the social system in the project environment. The ambient social structure may be such that certain categories of workers may be in short supply or nonexistent. The effect of the project on the social status of the project participants must be assessed to ensure compatibility. It should be recognized that workers in certain industries may have certain status symbols within the society.

Safety feasibility: Safety feasibility is another important aspect that should be considered in project planning. Safety feasibility refers to an analysis of whether the project is capable of being implemented and operated safely with minimal adverse effects on the environment. Unfortunately, environmental impact assessment is often not adequately addressed in complex projects. As an example, the North America Free Trade Agreement (NAFTA) between the U.S., Canada, and Mexico was temporarily suspended in 1993 because of the legal consideration of the potential environmental impacts of the projects to be undertaken under the agreement.

Political feasibility: A politically feasible project may be referred to as a "politically correct project." Political considerations often dictate the direction for a proposed project. This is particularly true for large projects with national visibility that may have significant government inputs and political implications. For example, political necessity may be a source of support for a project regardless of the project's merits. On the other hand, worthy projects may face insurmountable opposition simply because of political factors. Political feasibility analysis requires an evaluation of the compatibility of project goals with the prevailing goals of the political system.

Family feasibility: As long as we, as human beings, belong within some family setting, whether immediate family or extended relatives, family feasibility should be one of the dimensions of the overall feasibility of a project. This is not normally addressed in conventional project feasibility analysis. But this author believes that it is important enough to be included as an explicit requirement. For example, a decision to move from one city to another for the purpose of starting a new corporate job should be made with respect to family needs, desires, and preferences.

Project Need analysis: This indicates recognition of a need for the project. The need may affect the organization itself, another organization, the public, or the government. A preliminary study is conducted to confirm and evaluate the need. A proposal of how the need may be satisfied is then made. Pertinent questions that should be asked include the following:

- Is the need significant enough to justify the proposed project?
- Will the need still exist by the time the project is completed?
- What are alternate means of satisfying the need?
- What are the economic, social, environmental, and political impacts of the need?

It is essential to identify and resolve conflicts in project planning early before resources are committed to work elements that do not add value to the final goal of a project.

Chapter Six

Communication, Cooperation, and Coordination

Communication is the root of everything else.

================

Communication, cooperation, and coordination are essential for getting things done, even where no other participants are involved. It is often said that one should listen to the inner voice. Well, that is, indeed, an example of self-communication. Similarly, self awareness is an example of self-cooperation. Furthermore, being organized means being well self-coordinated.

Organizations thrive by investing in three primary resources as outlined below:

- The **People** who do the work,
- The **Tools** that the people use to do the work,
- and The **Process** that governs the work that the people do

Of the three, investing in people is the easiest thing an organization can do and we should do it whenever we have an opportunity. The Triple C model of project management is shown in Figure 6.1. The model incorporates the qualitative (human) aspects of a project into overall project requirements.

The Triple C model is effective for project control. The model states that project management can be enhanced by implementing it within the integrated functions summarized below:

- Communication
- Cooperation
- Coordination

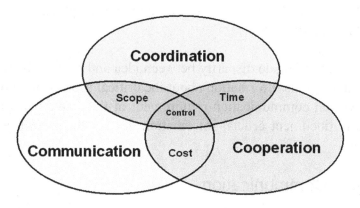

Figure 6.1: Triple C Model of Project Management

The Triple C model facilitates a systematic approach to project planning, organizing, scheduling, and control. The Triple C model can be implemented for project planning, scheduling and control purposes for any type of project. Each project element requires effective communication, sustainable cooperation, and adaptive coordination.

The basic questions of what, who, why, how, where, and when revolve around the Triple C model. It highlights what must be done and when. It can also help to identify the resources (personnel, equipment, facilities, etc.) required for each effort through communication and coordination processes. It points out important questions such as the following:

- Does each project participant know what the objective is?
- Does each participant know his or her role in achieving the objective?

- What obstacles may prevent a participant from playing his or her role effectively?

Triple C can mitigate disparity between idea and practice because it explicitly solicits information about the critical aspects of a project. The written communication requirement of the Triple C approach helps to document crucial information needed for project control later on.

Project Communication

Communication makes is possible for people to work together. The communication function in any project effort involves making all those concerned become aware of project requirements and progress. Those who will be affected by the project directly or indirectly, as direct participants or as beneficiaries, should be informed as appropriate regarding the following:

- Scope of the project
- Personnel contribution required
- Expected cost and merits of the project
- Project organization and implementation plan
- Potential adverse effects if the project should fail
- Alternatives, if any, for achieving the project goal
- Potential direct and indirect benefits of the project

The communication channel must be kept open throughout the project life cycle. In addition to internal communication, appropriate external sources should also be consulted. The project manager must

- Exude commitment to the project
- Utilize the communication responsibility matrix
- Facilitate multi-channel communication interfaces
- Identify internal and external communication needs
- Resolve organizational and communication hierarchies
- Encourage both formal and informal communication links

Types of Communication

- Verbal
- Written
- Body language
- Visual tools (e.g., graphical tools)
- Sensual (Use of all five senses: sight, smell, touch, taste, hearing:- olfactory, tactile, auditory)
- Simplex (unidirectional)
- Half-duplex (bi-directional with time lag)
- Full-duplex (real-time dialogue)
- One-on-one
- One-to-many
- Many-to-one

Project Cooperation

The cooperation of the project personnel must be explicitly elicited. Merely voicing consent for a project is not enough assurance of full cooperation. The participants and beneficiaries of the project must be convinced of the merits of the project. Some of the factors that influence cooperation in a project environment include personnel requirements, resource requirements, budget limitations, past experiences, conflicting priorities, and lack of uniform organizational support. A structured approach to seeking cooperation should clarify the following:

- Cooperative efforts required
- Precedents for future projects
- Implication of lack of cooperation
- Criticality of cooperation to project success
- Organizational impact of cooperation
- Time frame involved in the project
- Rewards of good cooperation

Types of Cooperation

Cooperation is a basic virtue of human interaction. More projects fail due to a lack of cooperation and commitment than any other project factors. To secure and retain the cooperation of project participants, you must elicit a positive first reaction to the project. The most positive aspects of a project should be the first items of project communication. For project management, there are different types of cooperation that should be understood.

Functional cooperation: This is cooperation induced by the nature of the functional relationship between two groups. The two groups may be required to perform related functions that can only be accomplished through mutual cooperation.

Social cooperation: *If we work together, we will grow together.* Social cooperation implies collaboration to pursue a common goal. This is the type of cooperation effected by the social relationship between two groups. The prevailing social relationship motivates cooperation that may be useful in getting project work done. Thus, everyone succeeds as a part of the group.

Legal cooperation: Legal cooperation is the type of cooperation that is imposed through some authoritative requirement. In this case, the participants may have no choice other than to cooperate.

Administrative cooperation: This is cooperation brought on by administrative requirements that make it imperative that two groups work together on a common goal.

Associative cooperation: This type of cooperation may also be referred to as collegiality. The level of cooperation is determined by the association that exists between two groups.

Proximity cooperation: Cooperation due to the fact that two groups are geographically close is referred to as proximity cooperation. Being close makes it imperative that the two groups work together.

Dependency cooperation: This is cooperation caused by the fact that one group depends on another group for some important aspect. Such dependency is usually of a mutual two-way nature. One group depends on the other for one thing while the latter group depends on the former for some other thing.

Imposed cooperation: In this type of cooperation, external agents must be employed to induced cooperation between two groups. This is applicable for cases where the two groups have no natural reason to cooperate. This is where the approaches presented earlier for seeking cooperation can became very useful.

Lateral cooperation: Lateral cooperation involves cooperation with peers and immediate associates. Lateral cooperation is often easy to achieve because existing lateral relationships create an environment that is conducive for project cooperation.

Vertical cooperation: Vertical or hierarchical cooperation refers to cooperation that is implied by the hierarchical structure of the project. For example, subordinates are expected to cooperate with their vertical superiors.

Whichever type of cooperation is available in a project environment; the cooperative forces should be channeled toward achieving project goals. Documentation of the prevailing level of cooperation is useful for winning further support for a project. Clarification of project priorities will facilitate personnel cooperation. Relative priorities of multiple projects should be specified so that a priority to one person is also a priority to all groups within the organization. One of the best times to seek and obtain cooperation is during holiday periods when most people are in festive and receptive mood. Some guidelines for securing cooperation for most projects are

- Establish achievable goals for the project.
- Clearly outline the individual commitments required.
- Integrate project priorities with existing priorities.
- Eliminate the fear of job loss due to automation.
- Anticipate and eliminate potential sources of conflict.
- Use an open-door policy to address project grievances.
- Remove skepticism by documenting the merits of the project.

Cooperation falls in several different categories. Some have physical sources, some have emotional sources, and some have psychological sources. The most common categories of cooperation include the following:

Project Coordination

After communication and cooperation functions have successfully been initiated, the efforts of the project personnel must be coordinated. Coordination facilitates harmonious organization of project efforts. The construction of a responsibility chart can be very helpful at this stage. A responsibility chart is a matrix consisting of columns of individual or functional departments and rows of required actions. Cells within the matrix are filled with relationship codes that indicate who is responsible for what. The matrix helps avoid neglecting crucial communication requirements and obligations. It can help resolve questions such as

- Who is to do what?
- How long will it take?
- Who is to inform whom of what?
- Whose approval is needed for what?
- Who is responsible for which results?
- What personnel interfaces are required?
- What support is needed from whom and when?

Types of Coordination

- Teaming
- Delegation
- Supervision

- Partnership
- Token-passing
- Baton hand-off

Through communication, cooperation, and coordination, we can offer a ***helping hand*** to our colleagues, friends, and team members so as to get our objectives accomplished. One good turn deserves another. As we succeed together with one project, so we shall succeed with another mutual project.

Communicate with all to get everyone's cooperation so that
coordination can happen

Chapter Seven

Project Planning

A plan is the map of the wise.

═══════════════════════════════

The key to a successful project is good planning. Project planning provides the basis for the initiation, implementation, and termination of a project, setting guidelines for specific project objectives, project structure, tasks, milestones, personnel, cost, equipment, performance, and problem resolution. The question of whether or not the project is needed at all should be addressed in the planning phase of new projects, as well as an analysis of what is needed and what is available. The availability of technical expertise within the organization and outside the organization should be reviewed. If subcontracting is needed, the nature of the contracts should undergo a thorough analysis. The "make", "buy", "lease", "sub-contract," or "do-nothing" alternatives should be compared as a part of the project planning process. In the initial stage of project planning, both the internal and external factors that influence the project should be determined and given priority weights. Examples of internal influences on project plans include:

- Infrastructure
- Project scope
- Labor relations
- Project location
- Project leadership
- Organizational goal
- Management approach
- Technical manpower supply
- Resource and capital availability.

In addition to internal factors, project plans can be influenced by external factors. An external factor may be the sole instigator of a project, or it may manifest itself in combination with other external and internal factors. Such external factors include the following:

- Public needs
- Market needs
- National goals
- Industry stability
- State of technology
- Industrial competition
- Government regulations.

Strategic planning decisions may be divided into three strategy levels: supra-level planning, macro-level planning, and micro-level planning:

Supra-level Planning: Planning at this level deals with the big picture of how the project fits the overall and long-range organizational goals. Questions faced at this level concern potential contributions of the project to the welfare of the organization, the effect on the depletion of company resources, required interfaces with other projects within and outside the organization, risk exposure, management support for the project, concurrent projects, company culture, market share, shareholder expectations, and financial stability.

Macro-level Planning: Planning decisions at this level address the overall planning within the project boundary. The scope of the project and its operational interfaces should be addressed at this level. Questions faced at the macro level include goal definition, project scope, the availability of qualified personnel and resources, project policies, communication interfaces, budget requirements, goal interactions, deadlines, and conflict-resolution strategies.

Micro-level Planning: This deals with detailed operational plans at the task levels of the project. Definite and explicit tactics for accomplishing specific project objectives are developed at the micro level. The concept of MBO (management by objective) may be particularly effective at this level. MBO permits each project member to plan his or her own work at the micro level. Factors to be considered at the micro level of project decisions include scheduled time, training requirements, tools required, task procedures, reporting requirements, and quality requirements.

Large-scale project planning may need to include a statement about the feasibility of subcontracting part of the project work. Subcontracting or outsourcing may be necessary for various reasons, including lower cost, higher efficiency, or logistical convenience.

Resolving Project Conflicts

Project conflicts should be resolved promptly and amicably. The Triple C model presented earlier is effective in resolving project conflicts because it is based on clear communication and mutual cooperation. Directional conflicts can mislead participants and stakeholders of a project. To bring everything into alignment, all concerned must see the project from the same point of view. The directional sign above shows the conflict of "one way" versus "my way."

When implemented as an integrated process, the Triple C model can help avoid conflicts in a project. When conflicts do develop, it can help in resolving the conflicts. Several types of conflicts can develop in the project environment. Some of these conflicts are listed and discussed below:

Scheduling conflicts: Scheduling conflicts can develop because of improper timing or sequencing of project tasks. This is particularly common in large multiple projects. Procrastination can lead to having too much to do at once, thereby creating a clash of project functions and discord between project team members. Inaccurate estimates of time requirements may lead to infeasible activity schedules. Project coordination can help avoid schedule conflicts.

Cost conflicts: Project cost may not be generally acceptable to the clients of a project. This will lead to project conflict. Even if the initial cost of the project is acceptable, a lack of cost control during project implementation can lead to conflicts. Poor budget allocation approaches and the lack of financial feasibility study will cause cost conflicts later on in a project. Communication and coordination can help prevent most of the adverse effects of cost conflicts.

Performance conflicts: If clear performance requirements are not established, performance conflicts will develop. A lack of clearly defined performance standards can lead each person to evaluate his or her own performance based on personal value judgments. In order to uniformly evaluate quality of work and monitor project progress, performance standards should be established by using the Triple C approach.

Management conflicts: There must be a two-way alliance between management and the project team. The views of management should be understood by the team. The views of the team should be appreciated by management. If this does not happen, management conflicts will develop. A lack of a two-way interaction can lead to strikes and industrial actions which can be detrimental to project objectives. The Triple C approach can help create a cordial dialogue environment between management and the project team.

Technical conflicts: If the technical basis of a project is not sound, technical conflicts will develop. Manufacturing and automation projects are particularly prone to technical conflicts because of their significant dependence on technology. Lack of a comprehensive technical feasibility study will lead to technical conflicts. Performance requirements and systems specifications can be integrated through the Triple C approach to avoid technical conflicts.

Priority conflicts: Priority conflicts can develop if project objectives are not defined properly and applied uniformly across a project. Lack of direction in project definition can lead each project member to define individual goals that may be in conflict with the intended goal of a project. Lack of consistency of project mission is another potential source of priority conflicts. Over-assignment of responsibilities with no guidelines for relative significance levels can also lead to priority conflicts. Communication can help defuse priority conflicts.

Resource Conflicts: Resource allocation problems are a major source of conflicts in project management. Competition for resources, including personnel, tools, hardware, software, and so on, can lead to disruptive clashes among project members. The Triple C approach can help secure resource cooperation.

Power Conflicts: Project politics can lead to power plays as one individual seeks to widen his or her scope of power. This can, obviously, adversely affect the progress of a project. Project authority and project power should be clearly differentiated: Project authority is the control that a person has by virtue of his or her functional post, while project power relates to the clout and influence which a person can exercise due to connections within the administrative structure. People with popular personalities can often wield a lot of project power in spite of low or nonexistent project authority. The Triple C model can facilitate a positive marriage of project authority and power to the benefit of project goals. This will help define clear leadership for a project.

Personality conflicts: Personality conflicts are a common problem in projects involving a large group of people. The larger a project, the larger the size of the management team needed to keep things running. Unfortunately, the larger management team also creates an opportunity for personality conflicts. Communication and cooperation can help defuse personality conflicts. Some guidelines for resolving project conflicts are presented below:

- Approach the source of conflict.
- Gather all the relevant facts.
- Notify those involved in writing.
- Solicit mediation.
- Report to the appropriate authorities.

Chapter Eight

Activity Sequencing

"There is time for everything, and a season for each activity."

- Ecclesiastes 3:1

===

It is important to sequence activities to determine the most effective order to execute them. This is referred to as activity sequencing, which is the key part of project scheduling. Even simple tasks at home such as cooking, doing laundry, house cleaning, and dressing up do require proper sequencing. The usual stress of multi-tasking to accomplish these chores can be mitigated by smooth sequencing.

Activity sequencing presents the interactions between activities and their precedence relationships. In order to develop an effective project schedule, the following questions should be addressed:

Which activities must come first?

Which activities must follow which ones?

Can some activities be run in series or parallel?

Can some activities be eliminated?

What type and level of dependency exists among activities?

Activity sequencing requires the following items:

1. **Project Scope Statement** – The Project Scope statement describes the characteristics of the project and boundaries of performance. The project scope statement complements the project charter.

2. **Activity List** – The Activity List shows the list of activities making up the project. Activity sequencing is the structural ordering of the activities in the list. Activity list is a breakdown of the project deliverables into their component activities, which provide crucial inputs for constructing the Work Breakdown Structure (WBS).

3. **Activity attributes** – Activity attributes specify the individual characteristics of activities. The attributes are important for scheduling, sorting, and arranging the contents of the project. Descriptions of activities often include activity codes, related activities, physical locations, responsible persons, assumptions, and constraints.

4. **Milestones** – Milestones indicate points of significant accomplishments in the project. They indicate progress toward the eventual goal of the project.

The common tools and techniques for activity sequencing are described below:

- **Precedence Diagramming Method (PDM)** - PDM is the most widely used network diagramming method for activity sequencing. It shows activity relationships as start-to-start, start-to-finish, finish-to-start, and finish-to-finish. Each activity is represented by a rectangular block, or node, and linked by arrows to show activity-to-activity dependencies.

- **Arrow Diagramming Method (ADM)** - ADM is a network diagramming method in which activities are shown as arrows. It is sometimes called Activity-On-Arrows. The application of ADM is limited to finish-to-start relationships among activities. The sequence in which activities should be performed is shown by joining activity arrows at nodes. If desired, dummy activities (dummy nodes) are included to indicate project starting point and overall ending point.

- **Dependency determination** - Determining the types of dependencies (i.e., precedence relationship) is critical to the development of a project network diagram. The three types of dependencies used to define the sequence among the activities are:

  o Mandatory (e.g., technical),
  o Discretionary (e.g., procedural preferences), and
  o External (e.g., imposed requirements).

- **Applying leads and lags** - Using leads and lags allows the logical relationships between activities to be accurately described. A lead allows for bringing forward the next activity or letting it overlap the preceding activity by a given amount of time. A lag allows for delaying the next activity by a given amount of time or project space.

Sequencing can be performed by using project management software, manual techniques, or a combination of both. The end result of activity sequencing is the network diagram that provides a graphical representation of project activities, milestones, objectives, goals, and the order in which they need to be accomplished. It is helpful to widely disseminate the network diagram so everyone can see and understand exactly where each person fits in the overall project scheme.

Activity sequencing results in outputs which assist in scheduling project activities, allocating resources, and assuring explicit documentation for the required project activities.

Question to ponder about pursuing milestones: Suppose you are 55 years old now. Would you embark on a personal project whose end result is not to be realized for decades to come? Why or why not? Consider the incremental gratification of accomplishing milestones along the way. Figure 7.1 shows the stages of activity sequencing for any project, spanning the cycle of planning, organizing, activity sequencing, project scheduling, tracking, and control. The cycle is repeated again and again such that the outputs of the control stage are used in subsequent planning functions.

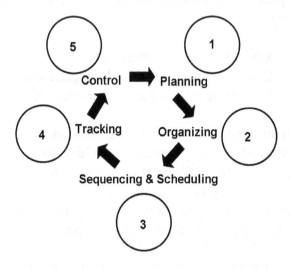

Figure 7.1: Activity Sequencing Stages

Activity Scheduling

Project scheduling is often the most visible step in the sequence of steps of project management. The two most common techniques of basic project scheduling are the Critical Path Method (CPM) and Program Evaluation and Review Technique (PERT). The network of activities contained in a project provides the basis for scheduling the project and can be represented graphically to show both the contents and objectives of the project. Extensions to CPM and PERT include Precedence Diagramming Method (PDM) and Critical Resource Diagramming (CRD). These extensions were developed to take care of specialized needs in a particular project scenario. PDM technique permits the relaxation of the precedence structures in a project so that the project duration can be compressed. CRD handles the project scheduling process by using activity-resource assignment as the primary scheduling focus. This approach facilitates resource-based scheduling rather than activity-based scheduling so that resources can be more effectively utilized.

CPM network analysis procedures originated from the traditional Gantt Chart, or bar chart, developed by Henry L. Gantt during World War I. There have been several mathematical techniques for scheduling activities, especially where resource constraints are a major factor. Unfortunately, the mathematical formulations are not generally practical due to the complexity involved in implementing them for realistically large projects. Even computer implementations of the complex mathematical techniques often become too cumbersome for real-time managerial applications. A basic CPM project network analysis is typically implemented in three phases:

- Network Planning Phase
- Network Scheduling Phase
- Network Control Phase.

Network planning: In network planning phase, the required activities and their precedence relationships are determined. Precedence requirements may be determined on the basis of the following:

- Technological constraints
- Procedural requirements
- Imposed limitations

The project activities are represented in the form of a network diagram. The two popular models for network drawing are the activity-on-arrow (AOA) and the activity-on-node (AON). In the AOA approach, arrows are used to represent activities, while nodes represent starting and ending points of activities. In the AON approach, conversely, nodes represent activities, while arrows represent precedence relationships. Time, cost, and resource requirement estimates are developed for each activity during the network-planning phase and are usually based on historical records, time standards, forecasting, regression functions, or other quantitative models.

Network scheduling is performed by using forward-pass and backward-pass computations. These computations give the earliest and latest starting and finishing times for each activity. The amount of "slack" or "float" associated with each activity is determined. The activity path that includes the least slack in the network is used to determine the critical activities. This path also determines the duration of the project. Resource allocation and time-cost trade-offs are other functions performed during network scheduling.

Network control involves tracking the progress of a project on the basis of the network schedule and taking corrective actions when needed. An evaluation of actual performance versus expected performance determines deficiencies in the project progress. The advantages of project network analysis are presented below.

Advantages for communication

- clarifies project objectives
- establishes the specifications for project performance
- provides a starting point for more detailed task analysis
- presents a documentation of the project plan
- serves as a visual communication tool

Advantages for control

- presents a measure for evaluating project performance
- helps determine what corrective actions are needed
- gives a clear message of what is expected
- encourages team interaction

Advantages for team interaction

- offers a mechanism for a quick introduction to the project
- specifies functional interfaces on the project
- facilitates ease of task coordination

Simplified Introduction to Activity Networking

Network analysis can become complex and intimidating. However, there are many commercial software tools and downloaded shareware available as aids for project network analysis. Fortunately, not all projects require elaborate network diagramming. Personal projects, in particular, do not need network analysis before they can be managed effectively. Project network components are described below.

- *Node*: A node is a circular representation of an activity.

- *Arrow*: An arrow is a line connecting two nodes and having an arrowhead at one end. The arrow implies that the activity at the tail of the arrow precedes the one at the head of the arrow.

- *Activity*: An activity is a time-consuming effort required to perform a part of the overall project. An activity is represented by a node in the AON system or by an arrow in the AOA system. The job the activity represents may be indicated by a short phrase or symbol inside the node or along the arrow.

- *Restriction*: A restriction is a precedence relationship that establishes the sequence of activities. When one activity must be completed before another activity can begin, the first is said to be a predecessor of the second.

- *Dummy*: A dummy is used to indicate one event of a significant nature (e.g. milestone). It is denoted by a dashed circle and treated as an activity with zero time duration. A dummy is not required in the AON method. However, it may be included for convenience, network clarification, or to represent a milestone in the progress of the project.

- *Predecessor Activity:* A predecessor activity is one which immediately precedes the one being considered.

- *Successor Activity*: A successor activity is one that immediately follows the one being considered.

- *Descendent Activity*: A descendent activity is any activity restricted by the one under consideration.

- *Antecedent Activity*: An antecedent activity is any activity which must precede the one being considered.

- *Merge Point*: A merge point exists when two or more activities are predecessors to a single activity. All activities preceding the merge point must be completed before the merge activity can commence.

- *Burst Point*: A burst point exists when two or more activities have a common predecessor. None of the activities emanating from the same predecessor activity can be started until the burst-point activity is completed.

- *Precedence Diagram*: A precedence diagram is a graphical representation of the activities making up a project and the precedence requirements needed to complete the project. Time is conventionally shown to be from left to right, but no attempt is made to make the size of the nodes or arrows proportional to the duration of time.

Figure 7-2 shows the graphical representation for AON project network. The usual network notations and coding are:

A: Activity Identification
ES: Earliest starting time
EC: Earliest completion time
LS: Latest starting time
LC: Latest completion time
t: Activity Duration

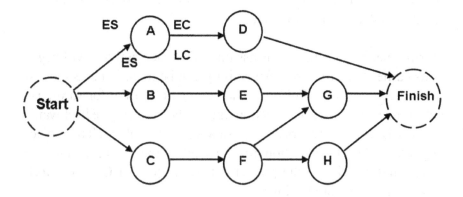

Figure 7-2. Graphical Representation of AON Network

Activity Precedence Relationships

As mentioned earlier, the precedence relationships in a CPM network fall into three major categories of technical precedence, procedural precedence, and imposed precedence. Technical precedence requirements reflect the technical relationships among activities. For example, in conventional construction, walls must be erected before the roof can be installed. Procedural precedence requirements, however, are determined by policies and procedures that may be arbitrary or subjective and may have no concrete justification. Imposed precedence requirements can be classified as resource-imposed, project status-imposed, or environment-imposed. For example, resource shortages may require that one task be completed before another can begin, or the current status of a project (e.g., percent completion) may determine that one activity be performed before another, or the physical environment of a project, such as weather changes or the effects of concurrent projects, may determine the precedence relationships of the activities in a project.

The primary goal of CPM analysis is to identify the "critical path," which is a determination of the minimum completion time of a project. The computational analysis involves both forward-pass and backward-pass procedures. The forward pass determines the earliest start time and the earliest completion time for each activity in the network. The backward pass determines the latest start time and the latest completion time for each activity.

During the forward-pass, it is assumed that each activity will begin at its earliest starting time. An activity can begin as soon as the last of its predecessors is finished. The completion of the forward pass determines the earliest completion time of the project. The backward-pass analysis is the reverse of the forward pass analysis. The project begins at its latest completion time and ends at the latest starting time of the first activity in the project network. Steps of CPM network analysis are presented below:

Step 1: Unless otherwise stated, the starting time of a project is set equal to time zero. That is, the first node, *node 1*, in the network diagram has an earliest start time of zero. Thus,

$$ES\ (1) = 0.$$

If a desired starting time, t_0, is specified, then ES $(1) = t_0$.

Step 2: The earliest start time (ES) for any node (activity j) is equal to the maximum of the earliest completion times (EC) of the immediate predecessors of the node. That is,

$$ES(i) = \text{Maximum of } \{EC(j)\};$$

for each *j* contained in P(i), which is the set of immediate predecessors of activity i.

Step 3: The earliest completion time (EC) of activity i is the activity's earliest start time plus its estimated time, ti. That is,

$$EC(i) = ES(i) + t_i.$$

Step 4: The earliest completion time of a project is equal to the earliest completion time of the last node, *n*, in the project network. That is,

$$EC(\text{Project}) = EC(n).$$

Step 5: Unless the latest completion time (LC) of a project is explicitly specified, it is set equal to the earliest completion time of the project. This is called the zero project slack convention. That is,

$$LC(\text{Project}) = EC(\text{Project}).$$

Step 6: If a desired deadline, T_p, is specified for the project, then

$$LC(\text{Project}) = T_p.$$

It should be noted that a latest completion time or deadline may sometimes be specified for a project on the basis of contractual agreements.

Step 7: The latest completion time (LC) for activity j is the smallest of the latest start times of the activity's immediate successors. That is,

$$LC(j) = \text{Minimum element of } S(j),$$

where $S(j) = \{\text{immediate successors of activity } j\}$.

Step 8: The latest start time for activity j is the latest completion time minus the activity time. That is,

$$LS(j) = LC(j) - t_i.$$

Gantt Charts

A Gantt chart is a special type of bar chart that shows a project schedule on a timeline. Gantt charts illustrate the start and finish times of each activity in a project. A project schedule is developed by mapping the results of CPM analysis to a calendar timeline. The Gantt chart is one of the most widely used tools for presenting project schedules. A Gantt chart can show planned and actual progress of activities. As a project progresses, markers are made on the activity bars to indicate actual work accomplished. CPM network and Gantt charts show the critical activities, which indicate areas requiring additional oversight and tight control. Figure 7.3 shows an example of a Gantt Chart. Figure 7.4 comically illustrates the importance of using Gantt Charts to avoid project problems.

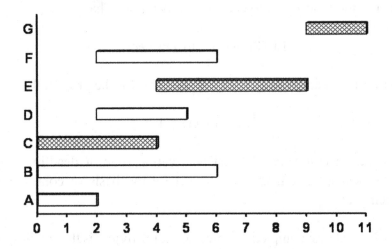

Figure 7.3: Example of Gantt Chart

Figure 7.4: Importance of Using Gantt Charts

Project Crashing

Crashing is the expediting or compression of activity duration. Crashing is done as a trade-off between a shorter task duration and a higher task cost. It must be determined whether the total cost savings realized from reducing the project duration is enough to justify the higher costs associated with reducing individual task durations.

If there is a delay penalty associated with a project, it may be possible to reduce the total project cost even though crashing increases individual task costs. If the cost savings on the delay penalty is higher than the incremental cost of reducing the project duration, then crashing is justified. Normal task duration refers to the time required to perform a task under normal circumstances. *Crash task duration* refers to the reduced time required to perform a task when additional resources are allocated to it.

If each activity is assigned a range of time and cost estimates, then several combinations of time and cost values will be associated with the overall project. Iterative procedures are used to determine the best time or cost combination for a project. Time-cost trade-off analysis may be conducted, for example, to determine the marginal cost of reducing the duration of the project by one time unit.

Time Management

"Do not squander time, for that is the stuff life is made of."

- Benjamin Franklin

Time is that universal dimension that forms the essence of everything we do. Time slips away too easily and it is irrecoverable. If time is not managed effectively, a project that has a time basis cannot succeed. Managing time implies eliminating fluff activities from the project schedule. The author's poem below conveys the importance of time as a limited resource.

The Flight and Direction of Time

What is the speed and direction of Time?
Time flies; but it has no wings.
Time goes fast; but it has no speed.
Where has time gone? But it has no destination.
Time goes here and there; but it has no direction.
Time has no embodiment.
It neither flies, walks, nor goes anywhere.
Yet, the passage of time is constant.

(©Adedeji Badiru, April 20, 2006)

Chapter Nine

Resource Management

Resource is the engine of performance.

═══════════════════════════════

Along with physical assets, you are the most important resource for your projects. Just as you would manage your project resources effectively, you must manage yourself effectively in order to be of use to your projects. From maintaining healthy lifestyle, keeping financially fit, and being emotionally stable to having positive attitude, you, as a resource, must be managed continually.

It is through the effective utilization of resources that project goals are achieved. If resources are aligned, we can achieve better efficiency, higher productivity, and more effectiveness. Here, "resource" refers to the manpower, tools, equipment, and other physical items that are available to achieve project goals. Not all resources are necessarily tangible. Conceptual knowledge, intellectual property, and skill can all be classified as resources. The lack or untimely availability of resources is a major impediment to organizational project efforts. Thus, resource management is complicated and can be affected by several constraints, including the following:

- Resource interdependencies
- Conflicting resource priorities
- Mutual exclusivity of resources
- Limitations on resource availability
- Limitations on resource substitutions
- Variable levels of resource availability
- Limitations on partial resource allocation.

Resource Planning

Project planning, in general, determines the nature of actions and responsibilities needed to achieve the project goal. It entails the development of alternate courses of action and the selection of the best action to achieve the objectives making up the goal. Since resources are needed to achieve project goals, resource planning is the pivotal process that determines what needs to be done, by who, for whom, and when. Whether it is done for long-range (strategic) purposes or short-range (operational) purposes, however, planning should address the following components:

1. *Project Goal and Objectives.* This planning stage involves the specification of what must be accomplished at each stage of the project. Resources constitute the primary inputs essential for achieving objectives as shown below in a flow statement moving from resources to objectives:

Resource → Activity → Process → Project → Objectives

2. *Technical and Managerial Approach.* This stage of the planning involves the determination of the technical and managerial strategies to be employed in pursuing the project goal.

3. *Resource Availability.* This stage requires the allocation of the resources for carrying out the actions needed to achieve the project goal.

4. *Project Schedule.* This stage involves creating a logical and time-based organization of the tasks and milestones contained in the project. The schedule is typically influenced by resource limitations.

5. *Contingency Plan and Re-planning.* This involves the identification of auxiliary actions to be taken in case of unexpected developments in the project.

6. *Project Policy*. This involves specifying the general guidelines for carrying out tasks within the project.

7. *Project Procedure*. This stage involves specifying the detailed method for implementing a given policy relative to the tasks needed to achieve the project goal.

8. *Performance Standard*. This stage involves the establishment of a minimum acceptable level of quality for the products of the project.

9. *Tracking, Reporting, and Auditing*. These involve keeping track of the project plans, evaluating tasks, and scrutinizing the records of the project. Figure 8-1 shows a performance-tracking chart based on resource availability over time. The dark areas of the bars indicate the portion of the expected performance that is in deficit. That implies that full performance is not always achieved from resource allocation.

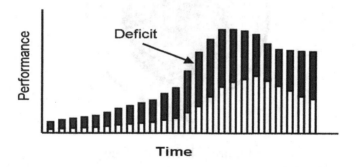

Figure 8.1: Resource-Based Performance Tracking

Chapter Ten

Economics of Getting Things Done

If money could just grow on trees . . . .

Economic and financial issues can impede or enhance project performance. Financial worries create distractions in a project.

If money grew on trees, as shown in Figure 9.1, we would always pluck some; and would have no need for money management within project management.

Figure 9.1: Money Tree

The time value of money is an important factor in project planning and control. This is particularly crucial for dynamic projects that are subject to changes in several cost parameters due to changing operating environments at work and at home. Both the timing and quantity of cash flows are important for project management. The evaluation of a project alternative requires consideration of the initial investment, depreciation, taxes, inflation, economic life, salvage value, and timing of expenditures.

Cost Management Definitions

Cost management in a project environment refers to the functions required to maintain effective financial control of the project throughout its life cycle. There are several cost concepts that influence the economic aspects of managing projects. Within a given scope of analysis, there will be a combination of different types of cost factors as defined below:

Actual cost of work performed

The cost actually incurred and recorded in accomplishing the work performed within a given time period.

Applied direct cost

The amounts recognized in the time period associated with the consumption of labor, material, and other direct resources, without regard to the date of commitment or the date of payment. These amounts are to be charged to work-in-process (WIP) when resources are actually consumed, material resources are withdrawn from inventory for use, or material resources are received and scheduled for use within 60 days.

Budgeted cost for work performed

The sum of the budgets for completed work plus the appropriate portion of the budgets for level of effort and apportioned effort. Apportioned effort is effort that by itself is not readily divisible into short-span work packages but is related in direct proportion to measured effort.

Budgeted cost for work scheduled

The sum of budgets for all work packages and planning packages scheduled to be accomplished (including work in process), plus the amount of level of effort and apportioned effort scheduled to be accomplished within a given period of time.

Direct cost

Cost that is directly associated with actual operations of a project. Typical sources of direct costs are direct material costs and direct labor costs. Direct costs are those that can be reasonably measured and allocated to a specific component of a project.

Economies of Scale

This is a term referring to the reduction of the relative weight of the fixed cost in total cost, achieved by increasing the quantity of output. Economies of scale help to reduce the final unit cost of a product and are often simply referred to as the savings due to mass production.

Estimated cost at completion

This refers to the sum of actual direct costs, plus indirect costs that can be allocated to a contract, plus the estimate of costs (direct and indirect) for authorized work remaining to be done.

First cost

The total initial investment required to initiate a project or the total initial cost of the equipment needed to start the project.

Fixed cost

Costs incurred regardless of the level of operation of a project. Fixed costs do not vary in proportion to the quantity of output.

Examples of costs that make up the fixed cost of a project are administrative expenses, certain types of taxes, insurance cost, depreciation cost, and debt servicing cost. These costs usually do not vary in proportion to quantity of output.

Incremental cost

The additional cost of changing the production output from one level to another. Incremental costs are normally variable costs.

Indirect cost

This is a cost that is indirectly associated with project operations. Indirect costs are those that are difficult to assign to specific components of a project. An example of an indirect cost is the cost of computer hardware and software needed to manage project operations. Indirect costs are usually calculated as a percentage of a component of direct costs. For example, the indirect costs in an organization may be computed as 10% of direct labor costs.

Life-cycle cost

This is the sum of all costs, recurring and nonrecurring, associated with a project during its entire life cycle.

Maintenance cost

This is a cost that occurs intermittently or periodically for the purpose of keeping project equipment in good operating condition.

Marginal cost

Marginal cost is the additional cost of increasing production output by one additional unit. The marginal cost is equal to the slope of the total cost curve or line at the current operating level.

Operating cost

This is a recurring cost needed to keep a project in operation during its life cycle. Operating costs may consist of such items as labor, material, and energy costs.

Opportunity cost

This refers to the cost of forgoing the opportunity to invest in a venture that, if it had been pursued, would have produced an economic advantage. Opportunity costs are usually incurred due to limited resources that make it impossible to take advantage of all investment opportunities. It is often defined as the cost of the best-rejected opportunity. Opportunity costs can also be incurred due to a missed opportunity rather than due to an intentional rejection. In many cases, opportunity costs are hidden or implied because they typically relate to future events that cannot be accurately predicted.

Overhead cost

These are costs incurred for activities performed in support of the operations of a project. The activities that generate overhead costs support the project efforts rather than contributing directly to the project goal. The handling of overhead costs varies widely from company to company. Typical overhead items are electric power cost, insurance premiums, cost of security, and inventory carrying cost.

Standard cost

This is a cost that represents the normal or expected cost of a unit of the output of an operation. Standard costs are established in advance. They are developed as a composite of several component costs, such as direct labor cost per unit, material cost per unit, and allowable overhead charge per unit.

Sunk cost

Sunk cost is a cost that occurred in the past and cannot be recovered under the present analysis. This is the most difficult cost element for consumers to comprehend and accept. Sunk costs should have no bearing on the prevailing economic analysis and project decisions. Ignoring sunk costs can be a difficult task for analysts. For example, if $950,000 was spent four years ago to buy a piece of equipment for a technology-based project, a decision on whether or not to replace the equipment now should not consider that initial cost. But uncompromising analysts might find it difficult to ignore that much money. Similarly, an individual making a decision on selling a personal automobile would typically try to relate the asking price to what was paid for the automobile when it was acquired. This is wrong under the strict concept of sunk costs.

Total cost

This is the sum of all the variable and fixed costs associated with a project.

Variable cost

This cost varies in direct proportion to the level of operation or quantity of output. For example, the costs of material and labor required to make an item will be classified as variable costs since they vary with changes in level of output.

Some projects are good in concept, but poor in execution, particularly when time, scope, and cost are factored in.

Chapter Eleven

Summary of Guidelines

Let this be your guiding light for getting things done.

════════════════════════════

Exercise Fairness

Exercise spirit of fairness at all times.

Use Concurrent Tasking

You may have to burn the candle at both ends to get more done.

Lighten Up

Lighten up and have fun while getting things done!

Exorcise Demons of Negativity

Overcome the insinuations of ANTS (Automatic Negative Thinkers). Negativity destroys hopes and aspirations

Mind-Over-Matter Works

If you put your mind to it (positively), you can accomplish it.

Practice Healthy Lifestyle

Maintain a healthy lifestyle. Good health is essential for getting things done.

Embrace Life-long Learning

Learning new things creates new and exciting opportunities for getting things done effectively.

Do it the Right Way from the Start

There are both straight and narrow paths to getting things done. The shortest path may be the quickest way, but it may be paved with sticky tar of failure.

Stake a claim to success, by starting early

Get an early start and get ahead of the project game.

Delegate

Be courageous to delegate where it is appropriate and to the right people.

Perform some tasks with team approach

Teaming helps to share expertise, responsibilities, and resources to get things done.

Minimize multitasking

Although popular in theory, multitasking actually creates more opportunities for errors and low quality of output.

Avoid procrastinating

Get on with what needs to be done; don't wait until the last minute. Making incremental gains on a task makes it easier to accomplish it without panic-button disruptions. Haste makes waste just as rush makes crash.

Prioritize

Prioritize and focus on the most important task at hand. Beware of time robbers.

Don't be a perfectionist

The pursuit of perfection is an impossible dream. Be realistic that there are limits to what can be accomplished.

Failure can be good

Don't be afraid to fail. Failure is often success turned inside out. Accept failure, if it comes, and learn from it.

Follow a plan, not a routine

Get out of a usual rote. Think and work outside the box to try new things.

Project Clichés

Declaration of a Project: Project management involves various interfaces within an organization. The exchange of information at each interface is crucial to the success of a project. The declaration below, the original source of which is unknown, takes a humorous look at the importance of information transfer and feedback in a project environment. The original composition has been modified here to fit the orientation of this book.

In the beginning there was the Project. With the Project, there was a Plan and a Specification. But the Plan was without form and the Specification was void. Thus, there was darkness upon the faces of the Engineers.

The Engineers, therefore, spoke unto their Project Leaders, "this is a crock of crap and we cannot abide the stink that abounds."

And the Project Leaders spoke unto their Unit Managers, "this is a crock of waste and we cannot abide the odor which abounds."

And the Unit Managers spoke unto their Sub-section Managers, "this is a vessel of waste and the odor is very offensive."

And the Sub-section Managers spoke unto their Section Managers, "this vessel is full of that which makes things grow and the characteristics thereof are exceedingly strong."

And the Section Managers spoke unto the General Manager, "the contents of this vessel are very powerful and will promote strong growth of the Company."

And the General Manager looked at the Project and saw that it was good. He, therefore, declared the Project fit for shareholders' consumption.

Project Management Proverbs

The stress of managing projects often calls for adages that aid project team members to see the lighter sides of their functions. The proverbs below represent a small sample of the various proverbs and sayings typically found in project management circles.

The same work under the same conditions will be estimated differently by ten different estimators or by one at ten different times.

You can bamboozle an engineer into committing to an unreasonable deadline, but you can't con him into meeting the deadline.

The more ridiculous the deadline, the more it costs to try to meet it.

The more desperate the situation, the more optimistic the project engineer.

Too few engineers on a project can't solve the problems; too many create more problems than they can solve.

You can freeze the users specifications, but you can't stop them from expecting.

The conditions of a promise are forgotten whenever the promise is remembered.

What you don't know is what really hurts you.

A user will tell you only what you ask about, and nothing more.

What is not on paper has not been said or heard.

No large project is ever installed on time, within budget, with the same staff that started it.

Projects progress quickly until they become 90 percent complete; then they remain at 90 percent complete forever.

The rate of change of engineering projects often exceed the rate of progress.

Debugging engineering systems creates new bugs that are unknown to engineers.

Progress reports are intended to show the lack of progress.

Murphy is alive and well in every project.

Peter's principle prevails in every organization.

Parkinson's law is every engineer's favorite.

Project Manager's Phrases

Project managers use insider phrases to convey ideas when dealing with project managers and clients. The phrases below offer hilarious interpretations of how project engineers communicate. A project manager must be able to read in between the lines to get an accurate picture of the status of a project. When a project is declared as being complete, it may mean that the implementation stage is about to begin.

Phrase 1: The concept was developed after years of intensive research.

Meaning: It was discovered by accident.

Phrase 2: The design will be finalized in the next reporting period.

Meaning: We haven't started this job yet, but we've got to keep the manager happy.

Phrase 3: A number of different approaches are being tried.

Meaning: We don't know where we're going yet, but we're moving.

Phrase 4: The project is slightly behind schedule due to unforeseen difficulties.

Meaning: We are working on something else.

Phrase 5: We have a close project coordination.

Meaning: Each project group does not know what the others are doing.

Phrase 6: Extensive report is being prepared on a fresh approach to the problem.

Meaning: We just hired three guys ... It will take them a while to figure out the problem.

Phrase 7: We've just had a major technological breakthrough.

Meaning: We are going back to the drawing board.

Phrase 8: Customer satisfaction is believed assured.

Meaning: We were so far behind schedule that the customer was happy to get anything at all from us.

Phrase 9: Preliminary operational tests were inconclusive.

Meaning: The poor thing blew up when we first tested it.

Phrase 10: Test results were extremely gratifying.

Meaning: It works; Boy, are we surprised.

Phrase 11: The entire concept will have to be abandoned.

Meaning: The only guy who understood the thing quit last week.

Phrase 12: We will get back to you soon.

Meaning: You will never hear from us again.

Phrase 13: Modifications are underway to correct certain minor difficulties.

Meaning: We threw the whole thing out and we are starting from scratch.

Phrase 14: We have completed an extensive review of your report.

Meaning: We have read the title page of your report.

Phrase 15: The drawings are in the mail.

Meaning: We are currently advertising to recruit someone to work on the designs.

Phrase 16: Your point of contact is currently on out-of-town assignment.

Meaning: The person you spoke with last week is no longer with the company.

Summary of Project Execution Philosophies

"Everything is possible for him who believes." – Mark 9:23

1. Success, you will see it when you believe it . . . . . .
2. You can get more done by doing less. If you tackle fewer things to do, you will get most of them done.
3. Just as prevention is better than cure, so is preemption better than correction. Anticipate and preempt sources of problems.
4. Know when to do what. Don't waste your daylight hours to do what you don't need daylight to do. In other words, "make hay while the sun shines."
5. What you can't do anything about, don't worry about. Worrying consumes time and keeps you from getting other things done.
6. Household junks accumulate to fill the available space. Strive to weed out unneeded junks in order to minimize non-value-adding junk-handling activities.
7. Plan, Execute, Learn, and Close projects.
8. Maintain a positive outlook. Things are never as bad as they seem. Even if they are bad, they could be worse.
9. Mind over matter works. If you put your mind to it, you can accomplish it.
10. Avoid ANTS (automatic negative thinkers) because they eat into your progress.

11. Accept and take risk. It is essential for accomplishing goals.
12. Recognize and ignore what you cannot change or accomplish. Focus on what you can change and do.
13. Never wait on work. Execute project schedule such that work waits on you.
14. Avoid "wait loss" by sequencing activities logically.
15. Embrace the concept of "everything in its place; a place for everything." It saves time when searching for tools.
16. Difficult times are the best times to embrace new challenges and learn new things.
17. Success is failure turned inside out. Learn and improve.
18. Keep things simple and focus on the fundamentals.
19. Measure and evaluate performance. It is the basis for continuous improvement.
20. Be proactive. Opportunity knocks, but it never enters on its own.
21. Create open communication channels and use them to achieve cooperation and task coordination.
22. It is crucial to use cooperative engagements in getting things done.
23. Take risk and go out on a limp sometimes. You cannot accumulate if you don't speculate.
24. Get all your facts before setting out to tackle unfamiliar tasks. Half of knowledge can be more harmful than no knowledge at all.

Project Guiding Philosophy

"A cheerful heart is good medicine."
                              - Proverbs 17:22

Be positive and cheerful in all your undertakings. Each challenge is an opportunity to thrive.

Projects are built on challenges; and we should welcome them.

It is through challenges that we make mistakes.

It is through mistakes that we learn.

It is through learning that we improve.

It is through improvement that we achieve project success.

Preemptive Tips for Personal and Home Projects

Managing a project is one thing, managing events that impede a project is another issue entirely. Little things that we fail to manage at home or at work can significantly impact project success. A good example is household chores. Proactive routine maintenance of household assets can preempt time-consuming worries and repairs later on. The time, thus saved, can then be used for more productive project activities be it at home or at work. Self-help guides are replete with tips on household management and home improvement. But such tips often focus only on the cost saving aspects as well as convenience of the home owner. In this book we extend those familiar reasons to include benefits of better project management within or outside the home. Time saved at home will be time available for accomplishments at work. Common examples of household tasks, whether you Do-It-Yourself (DIY) or not, include the following:

1. Change furnace and air-conditioning filters as recommended by the manufacturer. This preempts breakdowns that may cause worry time, repair cost, repair time, and diversion of efforts from productive activities.

2. Replace door locks when you move into a new house, especially previously owned homes. This preempts security issues that may impede productive engagements later on.

3. Learn location of main water cut-off. In case of water accident, prior knowledge of the location will save time and preempts the need to run around helter-skelter trying to solve the problem. This facilitates effectiveness and efficiency in responding to home emergencies.

4. Proactively maintain the family vehicle. Doing the manufacturer-recommended maintenance proactively means that you do it at your own convenience sans pressure. This preempts having to deal with emergency breakdowns which may occur at the most inconvenient times. Time, thus saved, can be diverted to more productive project engagements. The idea of "if it ain't broke, don't fix it" does not help effective project management because when it finally "breaks," all hell may break loose.

THE END!

About the Author

Adedeji "Deji" Badiru is an award-winning author, educator, researcher, and administrator. He is a registered professional engineer (PE), a certified Project Management Professional (PMP), a Fellow of the Institute of Industrial Engineers. He holds BS in Industrial Engineering, MS in Mathematics, and MS in Industrial Engineering from Tennessee Technological University, and Ph.D. in Industrial Engineering from the University of Central Florida. He also holds a leadership certificate from the University of Tennessee. He is a member of several professional organizations and author of several books and technical journal articles. He has served as a consultant to several organizations around the world and has received awards for his teaching, writing, and leadership. He has diverse areas of avocation. His professional accomplishments are coupled with his passion of writing about everyday events, interpersonal issues, social observations, and self-help guides. In this book, he brings the corporate application of project management to the general user and consumer level. He is a consummate user of the techniques of project management. He credits most of his professional and personal accomplishments to using project management processes in whatever he does. He strongly believes that others can derive similar benefits from project management. Enjoy the book!